AWAKE

AT THE WHEEL

Awake

AT THE

Wheel

TOWARD A MORE

MEANINGFUL

MITZVAH OBSERVANCE

MOSHE M. EISEMANN

Rabbi Moshe M. Eisemann
403 Yeshiva Lane, Apt. 1B
Baltimore, MD 21208
(410) 484-7396

Designed by Misha Beletsky

Edited by Adina Gewirtz

This book was set in
Adobe Brioso Pro and Narkiss Classic MFO

ISBN 978-0-9817642-4-5

2 4 6 8 10 9 7 5 3 1

Printed in the USA

Contents

Introduction

WHAT DOES THE RIBONO SHEL OLAM WANT FROM US?

*C*ome join me on a tour through some very significant parts of our *Yiddishkeit*. Here is why I want to take this trip.* I have a gnawing feeling—actually it is more than that, I know clearly and absolutely—that my Jewish life is deficient on a very fundamental level. I would like to find out what I need to do to get back to where I would love to be.

Here is how I know that somewhere, somehow, I went badly wrong. At Sinai the Ribono shel Olam (Lord of the Universe) promised us that if we would do our part, *If you will abide by the covenant that I made with you...*, we would become a *Kingdom of kohanim* and a *holy nation*. Now it is hard to know what precisely these terms mean and how they work themselves out in practice. But Rashi renders *kohanim* as *sarim*, princes, so in some way Judaism appears to demand that we all become part of a very special aristocracy. Then there is the matter of the *holy nation*; we all have some idea of what a *holy nation* might look like, but actually getting there is more problematic. Now, I try to observe the *mitzvos* but, with the best will in the world, I cannot look upon myself as a Jewish aristocrat, nor can I describe myself as holy.** For me, the system does not seem to be working quite as it should.

I wonder why.

It occurred to me that quite possibly I was making the same mistake that many of us make when we buy complicated ma-

---

* If what I am about to say holds true for you, too, I am pretty sure that you would want to come along.

** Of course all of us have *kedushas Yisrael*, the "holy" status of being Jewish, simply by having been born from a Jewish mother or having gone through a valid *geirus*. However, something tells me that to qualify for the sanctity implied in a *holy nation*, something more is required.

chinery and then end up frustrated because we have failed to read the owner's manual. I know that this is not a particularly good metaphor. *Yiddishkeit* is not a Mixmaster and the rote process of pushing buttons is not going to get us closer to the Ribono shel Olam. Still there are similarities. There may not be buttons, but there are "buttons"—thoughts that need to be thought and experiences that must be really *experienced* if our performance of the *mitzvos* is to have the intended impact.

So for me and those of you who feel yourselves to be floundering in the same quandary as mine, it is back to the "owner's manual." I think that I can promise you an invigorating read.

Here is our first query. How did the Ribono shel Olam plan that the national and individual life of His chosen people should be lived?

Here is Devarim 10:12–13.

12. Now, O Israel, what does HaShem your God demand of you? [He asks only] *that you fear HaShem your God,* [so that you will] *go in all His ways,* [which will lead you] *to love Him* and *to serve HaShem your God with all your heart and with all your soul.*
13. [Which, in turn will help you] *to observe the commandments of HaShem and His decrees that I command you this day.* [All this is demanded of you] so that things may go well with you.*

The Ribono shel Olam appears to have hefty expectations from us. So why does He downplay the amount of effort we

---

* My rendering of these two verses is more a paraphrase than a translation. The phrases in the brackets are not reflected in the text. In addition, you may notice that instead of italicizing the various components in one unbroken line, as I would normally do, I italicized each of the various units separately. My purpose in doing what I did was to reflect the way that R. Samson Raphael Hirsch interprets this text. He argues that the *trop* (cantillation) yields that *to go in all His ways, to love Him, to serve HaShem,* and *to observe His commandments* are not separate requirements but that they all result from being God-fearing.

This reading of the text will be significant when we get to the *sugia* (section) from Berachos 33b that we will be discussing in the body of the chapter.

will need to invest by using language (*He asks only...*) that seems to imply that it is all really quite simple?

The Gemara (Berachos 33b) is as shocked as we are: *Is it then so easy to acquire yir'ah?* We share the perplexity of the questioner. A lifetime of shattered dreams, of sweet intentions ending up in sour disappointment and frustration,* bears out his question. In this matter we are all experts. Few worthwhile accomplishments are easy to come by. Very, very emphatically, *yir'ah* is not among them.[1]

If we empathize with the questioner, we are utterly stumped by the answer. Here it is: [You are quite right. *Yir'ah* is fiendishly hard to attain. But you must remember who is speaking here. It is Moshe Rabbeinu. And] for Moshe Rabbeinu it is indeed *a matter that requires only negligible effort.* Does *that* make sense? What could Moshe Rabbeinu have been thinking? Did he not realize that his own unique circumstances would make his own, his *very* own, experience utterly incomprehensible, and therefore useless, to his audience?**

Here is R. Aaron Kotler's answer to this conundrum:***

The simple meaning of the statement that for Moshe the acquisition of *yir'ah* required only minimal exertion is this: For anyone steeped in Torah it really does become a lot easier. Torah purifies, Torah sanctifies, Torah gets us where we need to get. [Accordingly, the word "Moshe" in the phrase, *for "Moshe" the acquisition of yir'ah required only minimum exertion,* needs to be put in quotes. For a "Moshe," one whose very being is defined by the Torah that he has absorbed, the attainment of *yir'ah* is really not so hard.] Moshe Rabbeinu's message did indeed have universal application. Become steeped in Torah and you will have an easier task of it.

---

* Please note that a high percentage of Weight Watchers clientele is repeat business. Good intentions are harder to live by than to give up on.

** Said the gold medal winner at the Olympics, "It's really no big deal. Anybody could do it."

*** Mishnas R. Aharon, 1, *Ma'amarim VeSichos Mussar*, 1.

Well, everyone can now breathe easy. We have a simple solution to all our difficulties. All we have to do is to become a living *sefer Torah* and everything else will fall into place.

Here I can see a lot of you readers smiling ruefully. I am sure that many of you will be asking as I did: *Is it then so easy to become a living* sefer Torah? And the answer, of course, lies readily to hand: *Sure, it is no problem at all. For R. Aaron Kotler it is really quite simple!*

Where do the rest of us come in?

Here is what I believe to be the answer. If it sounds a little (or, very) strange, why not check it out with your *rebbi* or mentor. I will not be offended if they disagree with the suggestion that I am about to make.

Let us try to come down to earth and see what all this can mean to us in real terms. I am going to assume that most of you people who are reading this book are not world-class *tzadikim* but that you are nevertheless serious about your *Yiddishkeit*. You would like to improve but you have heard many *mussar* talks about *yir'as shamayim* and have become scared, not so much of *"shamayim"* but of your own perceived inadequacy. I suspect that at some level you might be saying, "Look! I need to become better and I want to become better. But if that entails that before anything even begins to roll, I have to become a real *yerei shamayim*, one who really fears God, count me out. I know all about *yir'as shamayim*. The *Mashgiach*, R. Chatzkel Levenstein, was a *yerei shamayim*; the Steipeler Gaon was a *yerei shamayim*. That is not my league. *Es iz nisht far mir!* It is not for me!"

Please do not think that way. We are going to do some learning and find out that none of us are being left out in the cold.

Let us break down the message into some of its components.

He asks only that you fear...: Is the *yir'as shamayim** of which our passage speaks really the bugaboo that we make it out to

---

* Please note that I am using the expression *yir'as shamayim* although the *pasuk* speaks using the Ribono shel Olam's name—fearing God. For an explanation of this usage, see Maharal, Derech Chaim 1:3 (among other locations).

be? Is it really out of reach for most of us? Don't be so sure! It may be more accessible to us than we think. It is obvious to me that the Torah uses the term at a much lower voltage than that which we associate with the great *Tzadikim.*

My search program found the phrase *You shall fear your God* five times in *Chumash,* all in VaYikra. They are at 19:14: the prohibition against cursing a deaf person or putting an obstacle in the way of a blind person; 19:32: the obligation of acting respectfully to older people; 25:17: the prohibition against abusing people; 25:36: the prohibition against charging interest to a fellow Jew; and 25:43: the prohibition against forcing an *eved ivri* to do the kind of labor from which the Torah excuses him. It seems to me that the level of *yir'as shamayim* that is required for a conscientious observance of any of these *mitzvos* is well within the grasp of all of us.

And who is to say that the *yir'ah* mentioned in our passage rises above that standard?

So, if I am right, how does this modest pinch of *yir'ah* lead to all the wonderful results predicted by the *parshah?* I venture to suggest an equation that I believe, in its own context, is as significant as $E = mc^2$.* It is this: The *yir'ah* of which all of us are capable equals a serious attitude toward *Yiddishkeit, halachah,* and ultimately the Ribono shel Olam. Once we get serious, really serious, the Jewish world, so to speak, lies at our feet.

Is it then so easy to acquire *yir'ah?* Is *yir'ah* at the low voltage level that we are discussing difficult to attain? Is it in fact hard to be serious concerning *Yiddishkeit, halachah,* and, ultimately, the Ribono shel Olam?

Well, "Yes!" It is hard. But you will recall that Rav Kotler taught us that Torah can help. How much Torah would we need? What level of Torah sophistication would be demanded?

---

* I apologize. I could not resist that one. Please do not suspect me of trying to imply that I have an even vague understanding of Einstein's physics.

The time has come to address this question and I would like to offer the following thought.*

We have worked out that the *yir'ah* we are trying to stimulate is one that takes its *Yiddishkeit* seriously. How serious is that? Clearly it means very seriously, if it is going to move us along to this:

> ...that you will go in all His ways, which will lead you to love Him and to serve HaShem your God with all your heart and with all your soul.
> ...to observe the commandments of HaShem and His decrees that I command you this day.

It must be the real thing. Now, our thesis predicts that if we take our Torah learning seriously, things will not be impossibly difficult.

Well and good. Now, can one be serious about one's Torah without being a major *talmid chacham,* Torah scholar? I suspect that most of us are not major *talmidei chachamim,* so this is a crucial issue. *Nu? Can we or can't we?* My short answer is that I believe emphatically that we can. The following Chazal comes to mind.

> R. Yissachar taught that God takes delight in a person's learning even if it is unfocused and he jumps easily from one topic to another. The phrase ודגלו עלי אהבה (Shir HaShirim 2:4), which translates as, (Israel speaking:) *His banner fluttering over me speaks of love,* can hint (by transposing דגלו to דלגו) (God speaking:) *Even his leaps [from one place to another in his learning] bring Me to love him* (BeMidbar Rabba 2:3).

Or:

---

* Of course I can make no claim that this was the rosh yeshiva's thinking in the passage quoted above from the Mishnas R. Aharon. I cannot even say that he would agree with the suggestion that I am about to make. I offer my suggestion as my own thinking only and it should stand or fall on that basis.

Rav Acha taught: Even an ignoramus who reads "love" as though it were "hate," that is that he reads ואהבת, *and you shall love [God]*, as though it were written ואייבת (skipping the letter ה), which translates as, *and you shall hate* (−), deserves My love. Relative to him I will read ודגלו עלי אהבה as though it were written ודלגו עלי אהבה. Even his skipping the ה with its blasphemous implications bring Me to love him (Shir HaShirim Rabba 2:9).

Now it is perfectly clear to me that the Ribono shel Olam would not proclaim his love for dilettantes who fritter away their learning time simply because they cannot be bothered to do it right. Both Chazal must be speaking of people of limited gifts who are doing the best they can. If God loves them, then we can be quite sure they will meet Him in their Torah studies and they will learn to live in awe of Him.

The demands that the Ribono shel Olam makes of us are relatively simple but, at the same time, as we all know, they are very, very hard. The bridge that spans that fearful chasm is right there in front of us—with a warm sign of welcome, to boot. It asks only that, as we mature, we really mature. That is, that we shed our childish acceptance of what we are taught, the rote performance of countless so-called religious gestures that remain unexamined and un-understood, and start using our heads.

The simple Jewish life, getting up in the morning, saying *Modeh Ani*, washing *negel wasser*, saying the blessings that we are called upon to recite each day, and so on and on and on, offer stellar opportunities for many life-transforming insights about who we are and what we are supposed to be doing with our lives. But, if we are going to benefit from their magic, we are going to have to "push" the right "buttons." We do not allow our small children to fool around with our precious computers; we ought not to let the small children who are still hiding within ourselves to have access to the precious moments that are meant to shape our Jewish lives.

It is true that we teach our children *Modeh Ani* and all the other details that go into making our lives "Torah-dic." A *gezund oif zeir keppel!* But that is an exercise that is undertaken in the *chinuch*, educational mode. The *real* thing is meant for adults who not only act like adults but think like adults.

* * *

How do real, authentic adults act? What is "serious"? The answer lies in your local bakery. That is right; you heard what I said.

Why in the bakery?

Shemos 12:17 reads: *You are to carefully safeguard the matzos.* Rashi explains that the reason the *matzos* have to be so carefully watched during the baking process is that they not inadvertently become *chametz*.

The Mechilta has this to say concerning this phrase:

> Read *hamatzos*, the unleavened bread, as though it were written *hamitzvos*, the commandments.* Just as you need to make sure that the *matzos* do not become leavened, so you must make sure that the *mitzvos* do not become "leavened." This requires that when an opportunity arises to perform a mitzvah, make sure to do it immediately.

Apparently, we are being taught that just as leaven disqualifies *matzos*, so, too, does it disqualify *mitzvos*. What could this possibly mean? We have some idea what leavened dough looks like; it is bread rather than matzah. But what could possibly be meant by a "leavened" mitzvah?

We are not going to get very far unless we have a clear idea of what the function of leaven is when it is generated within the dough. Here is Wikipedia's description:

> A leavening agent is any one of a number of substances used in dough and batters that causes a foaming action *which lightens and softens the finished product.*

---

* Since our Torah scrolls do not come with vowels, this can be readily accomplished by simply adding another letter *vav. Here is how:* המצות changes to המצוות. You will agree that such a minor (imagined) change is not totally outlandish.

That definition is really made to order for our purpose.

"Do the mitzvah fast!" Chazal tell us, "and do not give it a chance to become *chametz*, to become *lighter* and *softer*."²

A command as it first hits us, issuing, as it were, from God's mouth, is lean and tough. Its message is, "Do!" And, moreover, since it comes from God, that "Do!" must be expanded: "Do with thought! Do in full awareness of the implications!" "Do so that your actions penetrate deeply into the depths of your being!" The command of the Ribono shel Olam deserves no less!

However, as time passes, these messages begin to sound less urgent. The sharp edge of immediacy becomes attenuated. The act turns from the whiplash order, the mitzvah with all that the term connotes, into a relaxing "good deed" that does nothing, or very little, for anyone.

In this book I want to share with you the results of my explorations into some of the bits and pieces of Jewish living that most of us do but not many of us think about. I began this chapter by bemoaning the fact that I feel neither aristocratic nor particularly holy. I am hoping that by becoming better acquainted with the whys and wherefores of what I am doing anyway, I will be able to get moving in the direction that I ought to be going.

Come, join me in my quest.

Together, let us try to grow into Jewish adulthood.

Prologue

*H*ere are some imagined headlines as they might have appeared in a *Gan Eden Gazette*.

REVOLUTION SHAKES OUR
PLACID GROVES
Consternation Is Reported
Among the Animals

Let us permit ourselves a little anthropomorphism* in order the better to understand the shattering impact that these headlines would have had upon the animals that were leading their peaceful and precisely structured lives in Gan Eden.

What happened? They are all being summoned so that Adam HaRishon could get acquainted and assign names to everybody.

I am trying to imagine how, let us say, a couple of antelopes might have been impacted when they realized what was going on. Here is what they might have murmured to each other.

"Who is this interloper? What does he want with names? Where does this ridiculous idea of attaching names to animals come from? All right, names are useful in pinning down

---

* Here is a dictionary definition of anthropomorphism: *Attribution of human motivation, characteristics, or behavior to inanimate objects, animals, or natural phenomena.* Please do not get me wrong. I am resolutely against the anthropomorphism that energizes many of the children's books that tragically make their way into many of our homes. The havoc that the Berenstain Bears and their ilk have wrought in the way that modern America looks at life is truly catastrophic. Still, I felt that just for a couple of minutes, we can use this artifice in order to generate the impact that these thoughts ought to have on us. There are, after all, innumerable midrashim that do this kind of thing.

definitions. But who or what would be interested in defining us? Each of us is what we are, responsible to no one but ourselves and our children, living by reliable instincts that never let us down. If, all of a sudden, names are going to play a role in our lives, that portends some very profound and significant changes. Who needs changes? Who wants changes?"

We must certainly have had some very worried antelopes here.

If someone would have pressed them to say whether the ideas of "good" and "bad" played any roles in their lives, they would have shrugged off the question. Of course there is "good" (that which will keep us alive) and "bad" (that which will hasten our death). But they would have pointed out that they never thought in those terms. In fact, they did not think at all in the sense that humans think. Instinct took care of everything; things were placid, predictable, and pleasant.

Let us leave the antelopes to their problems. It is time for us to get away from silly word-games and to become serious.

Please note that this chapter is not an attempt to come to grips with the story of the Tree of Knowledge and the tests to which Adam was exposed. Such an analysis is way beyond anything that I would have the right to undertake.

In this chapter, for reasons that will become clear as we go along, I am interested in the *nachash*.* I came across R. Samson Raphael Hirsch's treatment of this difficult concept and was swept away by the profound simplicity with which he dealt with it. I am going to share it with you and to use it as a springboard for the matters that I want to discuss in this chapter.

I am going to preface our discussion with two quotes from the Hirsch Chumash.**

The first comes from the commentary to Bereishis 2:16

---

* The word is usually translated as *snake*. We are going to stick with *"nachash"* because this creature has very little in common with the reptile we identify as a "snake."

** Taken from the Feldheim, Judaica edition.

where the Ribono shel Olam tells Adam that he is forbidden to eat from the "tree of knowledge of what is good and what, evil."

> The commands set forth in verses 16 and 17 begin man's training for his moral calling. It begins human history and it shows all future generations the path in which they are to walk. The interdiction against eating from the Tree of Knowledge is...not a rational prohibition. On the contrary, all the perceptive faculties given to man—taste, imagination, and intellect—oppose this prohibition. Man, with his own intellect, would never have decreed upon himself such an inhibition. What is more: even after the prohibition was expressed, he could find no reason for it—other than the absolute Will of God.

Our second quote comes from Bereishis 3:1 where the story of the *nachash* begins.

> The animals are truly "Godlike" in their knowledge of good and evil. They are endowed with instinct, and this instinct is the voice of God, the Will of God as it applies to them. Whatever animals do is in accordance with their instinct. For animals this instinct is Divine guidance operating within them. What animals do in accordance with their instinct is good, and any act from which their instinct restrains them is bad. Animals cannot err; they have only their one nature, whose call they must heed.
>
> Not so for man. He is to opt for good and shun evil out of his own free will and sense of duty. Even when he gives his physical nature its due, he must do so not because of the allure stimulated by his senses, but out of a commitment to duty. Even when he takes physical pleasure he must act in moral freedom. *Man must never be an animal.*

The antelopes were right to have worried. Profound changes were indeed in the wind. On the sixth day of Creation things changed irrevocably for them. They, as members in excellent standing in the animal world, would nonetheless become subordinate to man. He would rule them and he would use them. To use them well, he would have to know their nature. It became necessary to understand them, in short, to name them.

We have italicized the last sentence in the second Hirsch quote because it is the basis of all we hope to cover in this book. Much of the struggle that we are called upon to undertake in order to practice a meaningful Yiddishkeit consists of renouncing the undemanding world of instinct and, instead, making the extreme effort of engaging our minds. Indeed, we must persuade ourselves that man must never be an animal.

But we are jumping ahead of ourselves. This, after all, is only a beginning.

In the meantime, though, we can say that, as R. Samson Raphael Hirsch reveals to us, this short sentence underlies the entire confrontation between the *nachash* and humankind. We might go so far as to say that the *nachash* was telling the truth *as he, as an animal, saw it.* We might paraphrase his ideas as follows:

"Look, Chavah, I am speaking from experience. It is simply not true to say that in order to really know 'good' from 'evil' you have to have eaten from this tree. Believe me; I have dealt with good and evil all my life—I do so all the time. I have never tasted anything from that tree and nonetheless the decisions that I am constantly called upon to make are unerringly true. I know how to keep myself alive (good) and what to avoid because it poses danger (bad). So there is no reality in what God is telling you. 'Good' and 'bad' are very simple concepts. Everything that you need to know is defined for you by your instinct, which, by the way, is also planted in you by God. There is no reason to fear that by eating from this fruit you will die. The tree *looks* good (instinct) so it *is* good. The prohibition is simply a powerplay on God's part."

Was he right? Of course he was right—speaking as an animal. It was all a matter of definition. For dealing with "good" and "bad" as these terms have meaning in the animal world, nothing outside them is required. The built-in instinct works like a dream. The *nachash* did not realize, or if he realized, was determined to deny, that with the creation of Adam a different kind of "good" and "bad" had been introduced into the world. Morality had crashed into history and of what was "good" and "bad" under that frightening regime only the Ribono shel Olam, never instinct, was going to be the arbiter.

That is what the confrontation in Eden was all about. The *nachash*, as king over the animal world,* was making a stand against the changes that would disturb his hegemony if humanity were to take God's charge seriously.

The *nachash* refused to kowtow to the Ribono shel Olam. He was not about to tolerate a change in his autonomy.

The battle lines were drawn.

A LETTER TO MY READERS

Dear Reader:

Do you mind if I ask you a question? Please excuse my curiosity. Perhaps I sound like a *yenta*. If so, so be it.

Do you happen to know the *nachash*? Have you ever been accosted by him?

Do you have a conscience? Is it active or stuck in sleep mode? If you heard the Ribono shel Olam call *Ayeka?*—Where are you?—What would be *your* answer? Would you offer your address and perhaps even add your mobile number,

---

* See Sotah 9b: *God said, "I had decided that the nachash was to be the king of the animal world. Now, however, he will be the most cursed from among the animals."* It was apparently the *nachash* who was supposed to rule over the animal world. Because of the role that he played in the drama of the forbidden fruit, he lost that kingship.

It seems to me that it is boundlessly significant that his place was taken by the lion (Chagigah 13b: *The lion is the king among the animals*). The original king was apparently chosen for his intellect (*The nachash was the most cunning...*), his successor, for his brawn (*...strong as a lion [Avos 5:20]*). Even the animal world seems to have experienced a precipitous drop through the eating of the forbidden fruit.

or would you pick up the sheer terror of the implications living just beneath the surface of that simple question?

Okay, so you are getting angry at me. Who am I to go prying around like that and, anyway, what possible contact could you, an upright and serious Jew, have with, of all things, the *nachash*? Well, you are right on the first part; I have no right to ask you such questions and would not dream of doing so in a forum that would require you to answer me or anybody else. About the second part, I would counsel a little patience. Read on and reserve your reaction until you get to the end of this letter.

Let me ask you a personal question. No need to worry. Nobody, not I or anybody else, will ever know your answer. I assume that in the last twenty-four hours you bowed down at least three times as you were reciting *Modim* while *davening* the *Amidah*. Right? How profoundly were you touched on each of these three occasions? How life-altering were these three experiences? And, as long as we are asking some pretty impertinent questions, I will ask just one more. Were those bowings really "experiences" in any real sense of that word?

Here is why I am asking these questions. I want to get you to think about the affinity that [may] exist[s] between you and the *nachash*.

Here is a quote from Bava Kama 16a.

Seven years after his death, a person's spine turns into a snake. This only happens if, while he was alive, he did not bow down when reciting *Modim*.

What could this possibly mean? Here are some excerpts from the Maharal, *Nesivos Olam* 1, *Nesiv HaAvodah* 10.

It is entirely appropriate that someone who does not bow down when he recites *Modim* should "turn into" a *nachash*. There is a marked affinity between man and the *nachash*. Were there not, the *nachash* could never have had any type of contact with either Adam or Chavah.

...The act of bowing low before the Ribono shel Olam is symbolic of utter subordination. We bow when we feel ourselves to be in close proximity to Him. At that level of closeness there can "be" nothing other than He. Our approach to Him signifies our willingness to lay down our lives for Him, to nullify our entire being. The act of bowing marks us as His servant.

The *nachash* was absolutely unwilling to undergo such self-abnegation. He who does not bow down while reciting the *Modim* marks himself as a human *nachash*.*

And now, just to round things off, we will quote another piece of Maharal, this one from the *Chidushei Aggados* on the Bava Kama passage:

The reason that it is specifically the spine that "turns into" a *nachash* is that it is just the spine that most clearly expresses the affinity that exists between man and the *nachash*. The spine allows us to stand upright and it is just that stance that proclaims kingship. Originally the *nachash*, too, stood upright, since he, just like man, was royalty. Then came a test. Man passed, the *nachash* failed. To be deserving of royalty, one must be able to subordinate himself to a greater king; in this case the Ribono shel Olam Himself. Adam, the first *Ba'al teshuvah*, did just that and retained his standing of kingship. The *nachash*, by rebelling against God's command, showed himself to be unfit for the mantle. He was punished by losing his upright stance and having to spend eternity slithering along the ground. If man, *by not bowing while reciting Modim*, proves himself, *nachash*-like, to be insubordinate, it is fitting that his spine turn into a *nachash*.

---

* This, as also the rendering of the next Maharal to which we now go, are approximate paraphrases rather than any form of actual translation.

Think about this. If we could get ourselves to be interested in turning our often thoughtless genuflection into a real act of divine service, things could change pretty quickly in our lives. Don't you agree?

But doing this meaningfully and consistently requires an active and well-oiled conscience, one that will draw our attention to the fact that a puppet-like jerk taken perfunctorily without thoughtful self-effacement just because that is what we have always done will simply not suffice. You know why? It is because at bottom, deep, deep down where things matter very much, it stems from a noncaring that can only grow from practical denial.

Do you see where we are heading? Is there perhaps something of the *nachash* in us?

How are we to understand what kind of a creature this *nachash* was? I am no zoologist, but I am pretty certain that nothing like it can be found today.

In our sources the *nachash* is usually called *HaNachash HaKadmoni*, the original *nachash*.* Please look at the first footnote below and give the matter your most dedicated interest. This is very important material.

When the Ribono shel Olam created man, it was necessary that He also create a form of "anti-man," a creature that shared certain characteristics with man** but which, because of this commonality,*** stood in implacable opposition

---

* Please note that it is not *HaNachas HaRishon*, the first *nachash*. *Kadmoni*, *the original*, conveys the idea that we express with the prefix *ur*. *Nachash HaKadmoni* = the *urNachash*, the one that stands for all that can be subsumed under the name *nachash*, none of which can ever be an exact replication, but to all of which it is father and inspiration.

** See Sotah 8b: The Ribono shel Olam is speaking: *I had said, "Let him walk in an upright posture as do humans. Now that he has sinned he has lost that privilege, let him slither on the ground." I had said, "Let him eat the same foods that humans eat. Now that he has sinned, let him eat dust."*

*** The Maharal always returns to the assertion that in the absence of any commonality there can be no antipathy. What we have in common creates a degree of contact within which belligerence is possible. Absent such commonality, we would simply pass each other like two ships in the night.

to him.* The *Nachash HaKadmoni* seems to have been a one-time phenomenon that paralleled Adam HaRishon and was determined to find the soft spots in Adam's spiritual armor, thereby determining what kind of a person the "Adam" of history would be. Had Adam HaRishon remained untouched by his confrontation with the *Nachash HaKadmoni*, he would have kept the pristine purity and all-comprehending knowledge with which he had been created. He did not remain untouched and we all are witnesses to the results.

We are close to the end of this letter. It is time for me to apologize for the seemingly aggressive and offensive questions with which I opened it. Please believe me that I am very far from wishing to offend anybody, more particularly you, my friends, who are demonstrating your friendship by plowing through this impossibly long chapter. Here is my excuse. I was trying to catch your attention. I wanted you to listen carefully and meaningfully to the message that I am now going to spell out.

The Bava Kama passage that we have been studying should have a very sobering effect upon us. Obviously none of us can have any kind of an idea what "spines changing to snakes after seven years in the grave" might mean. That is not really important. I imagine that those who will pass the "Verher" (Yiddish for *test*) will find out once they learn Bava Kama in the *Mesivta shel Ma'alah* (the celestial Yeshiva). What we can and must pick up is the knowledge that the *nachash* is a baleful presence (at least in potential) in our lives. God forbid that we would ever be identified with it. But, the Gemara tells us, the possibility exists.

It all hinges on, of all things, the way we bow down at *Modim!*[1]

Earlier in this chapter we examined what was implied in that simple act. Let us assume that you who are reading this, as I who am writing it, have been merrily bowing away for years and years without any of these thoughts intruding upon us in

---

* This is not the place to discuss why this was necessary. For our purposes, we can simply take this as a given and move on from there.

the least. We probably had some vague ideas about thanking the Ribono shel Olam for the many favors that He does for us, although what bowing has to do with that was probably not clear to us; none of us do much bowing when we thank friends who did us a favor, but that is about it.

What did our conscience do about this unsatisfactory state of affairs during all these years? Except around the *Yamim Nora'im*, probably not much. Welcome to the *nachash* within us.

That is what this book is all about. It sets itself the task of strolling around our daily lives and checking off some of the simple things that we do all the time that could enhance our *Yiddishkeit* boundlessly if we gave some thought to what we are really doing.

Come, join me for the trip!

PART I

Drama in the Morning

1.

Modeh Ani

> Do not laze around when you should be getting up in the morning to serve your Creator. There is a lion inside you. Tap into its strength to help you do what needs doing. Ideally it should be you who "wakes up" the dawn. Do not let the break of day find you in bed (Orech Chaim 1:1).

*T*hese are the opening words of the Shulchan Aruch. Welcome to a dose of realism! If we are going to live Judaism's good life, to fight Judaism's good fight, we have, first of all, to get out of bed. There is great beauty in that simplicity.

How do we discover what we are called upon to do?

The siddur helps in a big way. If that is news to us, we really have only ourselves to blame. We just do not seem to care enough to grow much beyond what we did the day after we had our siddur party in first grade. We said the *berachos* then; we say the *berachos* now. Okay, that is a little harsh; it is true that nowadays we can handle the translations a little better. But there again, it is only a *little* better. If you are at all like I am, you probably lose many of the subtleties, the references where the real gold is buried, because you never bothered to learn the siddur as carefully as you learn a *sugia* in *Shas*.

Think this over and, I suspect, you will become aware of two rather dreadful truths: 1.) I am right, and 2.) that is pretty disgraceful. We seem to lavish more care upon our car mechanic when we try to get him to understand the pesky squeak that is scaring us, than we do upon the Ribono shel Olam rattling at the gates, so to speak, for us to let Him in.

Let us begin at the beginning.

Here is a quote from the *Mishnah Berurah* (1:8) based on *Seder HaYom*. The subject is the *Modeh Ani* prayer that we are called upon to say first thing in the morning. Please accept this translation for what it is: a very temporary (and rather awful) rendering that offers literal translations for the words, but that bears almost no similarity to the profound message that we will soon discover together.

Here, once more, I quote from the *Mishnah Berurah*.

It is best to say the following immediately on getting up:

I thank You, O Living and Eternal King,
For with great compassion have You returned my soul to me.
*Your faithfulness is all-encompassing.**

We are not yet ready for a comprehensive rendering. We are going to have to analyze the various wordings that are comprised in this deceptively simple little prayer very carefully. We will discover that it is absolutely shattering in its implications. It is hardly an exaggeration to assert that it generates a very powerful explosion that is able and ready to blast us into a day of true servitude to the Ribono shel Olam.

מודה אני לפניך...**: I think that most of us would be inclined to understand this phrase as expressing a sense of gratitude: *I express my thanks to You.* I believe this to be incorrect. Here is why. At this point, please take a moment to glance at endnote 1 in the Prologue to this volume, "Getting into the Spirit of the Book." There we learn that the meaning of the root י ד ה from which *Modeh, Modim,* and similar words are built,

---

* You will have noticed by now that I prefer paraphrase to translation. We simply do not talk the way the Hebrew is phrased. Either way, as we go along in this chapter you will find that I do not agree with this generally accepted understanding of the opening phrase, *Modeh Ani*. I hope you will stick with me. Exciting things are going to happen.

** I apologize to readers who are not familiar with Hebrew. I have tried hard to present everything in English throughout this chapter. However, the next couple of paragraphs require some analysis of the text actually used and some Hebrew words are unavoidable. Please be patient with me. This section will soon be over.

determined by the preposition with which it is used: *Modim al* (מודים על) is an expression of gratitude (I thank you *for*). *Modim sh*...(ש...מודים) is an avowal of a given truth (I avow *that*). In accordance with this rule, the correct translation of our *Modeh,* which comes with the ש (SH) preposition, (שהחזרת בי), would not be an expression of gratitude but an avowal of a fact. What fact would that be? As we work our way through the text, we will find the answer to this question.

שהחזרת בי נשמתי בחמלה: There are two components to this phrase. The first is *that You have returned my soul to me;* the second is, *with great compassion.* We will treat the two separately.

The prayer *Modeh Ani*...is not mentioned in the Gemara nor does it appear in the Shulchan Aruch. It is first mentioned in *Seder HaYom* by R. Moshe Ibn Machir,* who simply advises** that it be said in the morning but does not ascribe any source.

What did Ibn Machir have in mind when he ordained or suggested that we begin our day by contemplating the idea of the "returned" soul? The implications are truly shattering.

In the next chapter, when we think about the *berachah Asher Yotzar,* the blessing to be recited upon leaving the bathroom, we will come face-to-face with the fact that we humans are composed of both physical and spiritual elements. That is obviously not news to any of us. However, after we have agreed on this very general assertion, things get a little more complex. There is a question that is worth contemplating. How physical is our physicality? Are we literally first cousins to the apes as far as our bodily functions are concerned, differentiated from them only by the fact that the Ribono shel Olam "blew" a soul into us and not into them, or does this soul, this purely spiritual entity, subtly change our bodies as well?***

---

* He led a yeshiva in Ein Zeitim (near Tzfas) in the sixteenth century.

** His language, "Upon rising he should immediately say..."

*** Even at this early stage of our analysis, you might want to ponder the *Asher Yotzar* text. It reads in part, *Who has created* man *with wisdom....*Now the physical realities that are marshaled in this *berachah* to demonstrate God's wisdom are equally present in an animal's body. So why mention *"man"*? Think about it.

[Ramban to Bereishis 2:7 discusses this matter at length and considers both possibilities. I have analyzed this Ramban as thoroughly as I was able in my book *Beginnings* on *parshas Bereishis*.* Here we will assume the second possibility, that indeed with the entry of the soul into Adam HaRishon, even his physicality became sublimated to some extent.]

In the current context our interest is centered upon sleep. We sleep; animals sleep and some even hibernate. Certainly without Ibn Machir's helping hand, we would have been inclined to believe that these two forms of sleep are essentially the same. Here is what sleep looks like in a world that knows nothing of *Modeh Ani*:

SLEEP is a naturally recurring state of relatively suspended sensory and motor activity, characterized by total or partial unconsciousness and the inactivity of nearly all voluntary muscles. It is distinguished from quiet wakefulness by a decreased ability to react to stimuli, and it is more easily reversible than hibernation or coma. It is observed in all mammals, all birds, and many reptiles, amphibians, and fish. *In humans, other mammals*, and a substantial majority of other animals that have been studied...regular sleep is essential for survival.

Clearly, Wikipedia (the encyclopedia from which this excerpt is taken) thought it legitimate to bundle "humans" with "other mammals" in its contemplation of sleep. But for R. Moshe Ibn Machir's thoughtfulness, we would probably have concurred.

We asked earlier what he had in mind when he suggested that we begin our day with *Modeh Ani*. It has now become abundantly clear. A "Jewish" day is to begin with a "Jewish" awakening. Our sleep is more, much more, than a "state of relatively suspended sensory and motor activity." It is a daily meeting with the Ribono shel Olam Who delights in return-

* Chapter Four, "Of Brutes and Men." See page 25.

ing us to our bodies, cleaned and spruced up for another day of divine service.

This brings us to the question of *chemlah*, which we translated as *compassion*. What does this word mean in the present context?

Synonyms are a tricky bunch. They are close enough in meaning to make it easy for the careless speaker or writer to use them interchangeably, and, as long as we are not dealing with our holy language, no great harm will be done. In Hebrew, and more particularly in TaNaCh, such carelessness is, of course, absolutely interdicted. Each subtle inflection is Torah and losing that piece of truth would strike at the very heart of that which we treasure the most.

Here is an example from our own *sugia* to demonstrate how carefully words are chosen in TaNaCh. In I Shmuel 15:9 we have the tragic story of Shaul's disobedience when he did not destroy Amalek as totally as the Ribono shel Olam had commanded. The *pasuk* reads, *Shaul and the people took pity* (the word used is *chamal—ches, mem, lamed* (ח מ ל)—the root word from which "*chemlah,*" the word that we are discussing, is formed) *on...the best of the sheep, the cattle, the fatted bulls, and the fatted sheep and on all that was good, and they were not willing to destroy them.* There are two other root forms in Hebrew—*reish, ches, mem* (ר ח ם) and *ches, vav, samech* (ח ו ס)—that could be regarded as synonyms. Malbim takes the opportunity to discuss why *chamal* rather than one of the other two is used.

Here is a paraphrase of his ideas:

ם ח ר (*r-ch-m*) is inappropriate here because it can be used only between people. A person can be מרחם on another person; he cannot be מרחם on an animal. ח ו ס (*ch-u-s*) is used to describe the unwillingness to destroy something that could still be of use to the person who might otherwise destroy it. One is חס on his own property. ח מ ל (*ch-m-l*) describes an unwillingness to countenance wanton destruction. As a principle, it is wrong to destroy anything that could still have a purpose in life.

Both Maharal and R. Samson Raphael Hirsch appear to agree with Malbim's understanding of *chamal*. At *Devarim* 13:9 we are bidden not to be *chomel* on a *meisis*, an *enticer* who seeks to persuade people to serve idols. As Rashi explains, we are bidden to make no *efforts to find a favorable outcome for him*. To this Maharal in *Gur Aryeh* remarks: Do not be *chomel* means: *Do not feel sorry that this chunk of evil is going to be destroyed. In his case total oblivion is to his and everybody else's advantage.* Maharal is on the same page as Malbim.

At Bereishis 19:16 we learn how, when Lot had second thoughts about leaving Sodom, the angels grabbed him by the hands and dragged him out in order to save him. The text reports that these angels were ordered by the Ribono shel Olam to do this because God was *"chomel"* on him. Rav Hirsch notes that *chemlah* is always an *undeserved* favor. Lot had done everything wrong and nothing right. Still the Ribono shel Olam chose to save him. "To be" trumps "Not to be." Once more we have confirmation of Malbim's idea.

We are finally able to offer a rendering of R. Moshe Ibn Machir's *Modeh Ani.*

I affirm O Mighty King
That my awakening this morning
Has nothing in common with the awakening
Of the rest of the physical world.
That world simply moves from a state of suspended
Sensory and motor activity to one in which these activities
Are no longer suspended.
For me, waking up is a form of rebirth.
My soul spent the night with a loving, caring God
Who, because He feels the responsibility
Of returning it to me in the best possible way,
Spent the time refurbishing and cleansing it.
I am fully aware that on the basis of my past performance
I may not deserve this kindness,
But I know, too, that You prefer life to death,
existence to oblivion.
That You are willing to take a chance on me because

It is a better soul that You return to me this morning
Than was the one that I deposited with You last night.

Here the text ends, but the implications do not. If these were couched in a formal text they would read something like this:

O Mighty King!
I understand that the truths that I have now affirmed
Burden me with great responsibility.
I will gladly shoulder that weight.
I am about to wash my hands from a vessel[1]
Precisely as did the kohanim
When they were about to undertake their Avodah.
I am aware that I am a part of "a Kingdom of Kohanim"
And, by now, I have drawn the requisite conclusions
From that description.
I know that in the performance of Avodah
Inappropriate actions can disqualify
But so can inappropriate thoughts and intentions.
You demand a great deal from us, your ministrants,
But then by returning bright new souls to us every morning
You, too, have given us a great deal.
I understand O Mighty King, I understand.

* * *

May my humble efforts,
Offered in the spirit of all that I have now learned,
Find favor in Your eyes.

All this and perhaps much more would no doubt have appeared in this prayer if the implications to be drawn from our recital of *Modeh Ani* had been couched in a formal text. But they are not! Please note carefully and profoundly, they are not!

Why not?

I think that the reason lies in the fact that language, for all its wonderful gifts, also stilts and therefore limits. Imagine that having scaled a towering mountain, you stood at the summit with a vast panorama stretched out beneath you.

You felt—what? "Well," you stammer, "it was a certain something, something that I cannot really describe. All I can say is that it was a very, very special feeling." Imagine going back to school next day and having a shortsighted teacher asking you to write an chapter: *What I Felt Atop the Mountain.* You know very well that it simply cannot be done.

Modeh Ani, printed on the siddur page, conveys facts to our minds. As for the rest? That must remain locked in our hearts, finding release in actions and attitudes, never in words.

2.

Asther Yotzar

*T*here are different *minhagim* concerning the order in which *Birkos HaShachar* should be said, and everybody should, of course, adhere to the custom that is followed in his community. Our contemplation of *Asher Yotzar* and *Elokai, Neshamah* will assume the opinion of the Vilna Ga'on namely, that the two *berachos* form a twosome and that, in contrast to some customs, *Elokai, Neshamah* is to follow hard upon *Asher Yotzar.** The Ga'on's thinking is based on the Rema's opinion (Orech Chaim 4:1) that *Asher Yotzar* is to be recited in the morning even without having used the bathroom. The background to this reasoning is as follows. The *halachah* requires that, upon waking in the morning, we are to wash our hands in the particular way designated by Chazal for this type of washing. Rosh and Rashba disagree concerning the reason for this requirement. Rosh believes that it was instituted in preparation for *Shacharis*. While we were sleeping our hands may have come into contact with parts of our bodies that the *halachah* considers unclean, and accordingly a cleansing is mandated.

Rashba has an entirely different approach. Berachos 57b teaches that sleeping at night is equivalent to experiencing one sixtieth of death. Accordingly, we might look upon waking up in the morning as a mini-resurrection. Freshly brought to life, we are to consider what this life is all about. For us, the answer is clear. We are granted life so that we might be able to serve the Ribono shel Olam. Accordingly, just as a *kohen*

---

* It is preferable to say *Elokai, Neshamah* immediately after *Asher Yotzar*... (*Mishnah Berurah* 6:12).

31

has to wash his hands [and feet]* at the *kiyor* before the new day's service begins, so, too, do we have to wash our hands every morning as a prelude to once more beginning our personal servitude, the shouldering of the many duties toward God that our daily life imposes upon us.

The Ga'on sees the recitation of *Asher Yotzar* and *Elokai, Neshamah* as reflecting this quasi rebirth. Each morning, freshly minted, we thank God for both our bodies (*Asher Yotzar*) and our souls (*Elokai, Neshamah*). It is for this reason that these *berachos* are halachically considered a single twosome, and because of this, too, *Asher Yotzar* is to be recited in the mornings even under circumstances in which we had no need to use the bathroom.

After this introduction we are ready to begin our contemplation of these two *berachos*.

For *Asher Yotzar* we begin by considering Berachos 60b.

> Someone about to enter a bathroom addresses the following [to the angels who are said to accompany every Jew]:** "It is not fitting that you should enter the bathroom with me. Your honor, as also God's, demands that you remain outside. Leave me free to attend to my needs. It is what I want to do. Soon I will return to you."
>
> Abaye argued: He said, "Do not use this formula; [if this is what you say to the angels] they may leave you. Here is what you should say: 'I need your constant support. Please wait for me while I enter this place and then come back out to you. [Please understand] that this is something that humans have to do.'" ***

---

* Since our washing is no more than a reminder of what was done in the Beis HaMikdash, we are not required to go the whole distance. Our obligation is limited to washing our hands.

** Orech Chaim 3:1 notes that this exhortation has fallen out of use. *Mishnah Berurah* explains: "We are not so God-fearing that angels accompany us [let alone] that we may request them to wait until we finish."

*** I have used a paraphrase instead of a literal translation.

The following is to be said upon leaving the bathroom.
[The text of the *berachah* more or less as we know it is given all the way up to the final *Baruch....* Then we have a disagreement about what the wording of that ending *berachah* ought to be.]

Rav suggested that we should say, *Blessed are You HaShem who heals the sick.* Apparently, the need to evacuate the nonessentials of the food we eat can be viewed as a kind of sickness. Using the bathroom can be viewed as a cure for that illness.

Shemuel objects. Is it possible, or indeed desirable, to view the entire population of the world as invalids? Rather we should say, *Blessed are You HaShem who keeps our bodies healthy.** If the body wastes were to remain inside us, the entire ecology of the body would become distorted. It is not that this vulnerability makes us all into invalids. It is that were there no apparatus to make evacuation possible, our bodies would eventually sicken.

Rav Sheshes chooses a different route. He thinks that a different point ought to be stressed. Just as when a balloon is pricked, the air escapes, so, too, we would expect that our *ruach* (our soul) would be lost to us since a body riddled with so many cavities should be unable to prevent its departure. That it remains within us can be viewed as a minor miracle. R. Sheshes feels that this miracle should be acknowledged in the final *berachah*. Accordingly he closes with, *Who performs wonders.*

Rav Papa rounds off the *sugia* by suggesting a combination of the two ideas. The ending should read, *Who keeps us healthy and performs wonders.*

As does the Gemara, we shall begin by examining the two versions of the exhortations addressed to the angels who, if we only deserved it, would be accompanying us on our way to the bathroom. Obviously we will want to understand Abaye's almost vehement objection to the earlier version, but to my

---

* A paraphrase. Please see Rashi.

mind, it is even more crucial to have an explanation for the different expressions that the two versions use when they mention the evacuation of the body wastes that takes place in the bathroom. In the first version it is described with the words, *It is what I want to do,* while the second version chooses a much less suggestive term: *[Please understand] that this is something that human beings have to do.* Is it the tone of the exhortation taken as a whole that underlies the apparent change of attitude?

In my opinion the answer to this last question is an emphatic, "Yes!" There is no doubt in my mind that the two versions display radically different attitudes toward the very physical needs that are taken care of in the bathroom. The difference in language is an inevitable result from a profoundly diverging *Weltanschauung.**

The original version to which Abaye took such strong exception assumes a bifurcated** world. It maintains that, happily, there is much in our physical world that lends itself to sublimation, but there are also areas that do not. Among the latter, we must count a visit to the bathroom. On an average day there is much with which we can keep our accompanying angels busy, but the moment we enter the bathroom we put them on notice that, for a while, they will be off duty. We ask them to wait patiently for us to rejoin them. Once we do so, they will once more be expected to take up their tasks.

Abaye is absolutely horrified. There is no such thing as a bifurcated world. The hallmark of the Ribono shel Olam's relationship with us is *yichud* (unity). Nothing, but nothing at all, can be said to lie outside the purview of sublimation. Witness the fact that we have a whole chapter in our Shulchan Aruch (Orech Chaim 3) that deals with appropriate ways of acting in a bathroom. The angels are very definitely *not* off duty

---

* This is a German term that has made its way into English. *Welt* is German for "world." *Anschauung* is German for "a way of perceiving things." In combination we have "a way of perceiving the world."

** The prefix *bi* has the meaning "two." Think of the bi-cycle that describes a two-wheeler. *Furcat* derives from a Latin word meaning "fork." Thus bifurcated = *two-forked.*

while we attend to our needs; they never *will* be since there is
nothing that cannot be sublimated in some form; they never
can be since they are *mal'achim.*[1] The exhortation says only
that, since their sanctity precludes their entry into the bathroom,* they will, for that short time, have to exercise their duties from the outside. That is all.

The diverse expressions that we noted earlier fit perfectly
into their diverse contexts. If we are speaking of an area of life
that lies outside the sphere in which sublimation is possible,
then human predilections take over. We do what *we feel like
doing.* In Abaye's wording such a formula is unthinkable. Just
as the angels remain on duty throughout the procedure, so do
we. The service mode into which we entered as we woke up
and washed our hands* is in no way attenuated while we take
care of our bodily needs.

Let us now turn our attention to the texts.

Asher Yotzar is worded in the third person while *Elokai,
Neshamah* is in the second person.

Let us remember that in the previous chapter we decided
to base our contemplation of these *berachos* on Rashba's opinion that they are to be viewed as a twosome. Upon thinking
about this, it struck me as noteworthy that *Asher Yotzar* is
worded in the third person, while *Elokai, Neshamah* is in the
second.[2] Moreover, while, as we have just noted, the *berachah*
begins in the third person, it then, with the words *It is obvious
and known to You,* it switches to the second.[3]

I hope that you have taken the time to read endnotes 2 and
3. From the examples that I offered there, it is clear that neither of the two apparent irregularities that we noted in *Asher
Yotzar* is unique. Still, I suspect that, since in the vast majority
of cases consistency is the rule, we would need to explain each
of the exceptions in its own unique terms.

Let us think about the text of *Asher Yotzar.* We will get to
Elokai, Neshamah in the next chapter.

---

* Please see the previous chapter. Remember that we *pasken* in accordance
with the Rashba, as witness the fact that we say *Asher Yotzar* in the morning
even if we have not used the bathroom.

As a general introduction to our thinking, we should note that the Torah's grammar is far less rigid than our current, modern usage would consider normal. We cannot imagine an English sentence that reads, "Jack and Jill took." We would consider this wording intolerable since *to take* is transitive and thus requires an object. Nevertheless, we are perfectly comfortable with *"Vayikach Korach ben Yitzhar,* Korach the son of Yitzhar took," where no object to *vayikach* (took) is supplied. We know the Chazal that "he 'took' himself" and are happy to live with that. There is, of course, nothing wrong with that as long as we realize that this is not something that we expect in our daily speaking.

This same tolerance can be observed in the apparent inconsistency in the use of singular and plural in the same verse. I just opened *parshas* Mishpatim at random and immediately saw, *Do not* (singular) *pronounce the names of strange gods; let these not be heard from your* (plural) *mouths* (Shemos 23:13). Or, *Do not oppress* (singular) *a stranger; you* (plural) *know how he feels because you were strangers in Egypt* (Shemos 23:9).

Of course, in each of these cases there is certainly some good and sufficient reason for the irregularity. My point is that, in the hierarchy of values to which the Torah subscribes, strict adherence to grammatical logic takes a backseat when measured against the message that the Torah wishes to send to us.

Let us now take first things first. We wondered why in a twosome such as *Asher Yotzar* and *Elokai, Neshamah* are, one should be couched in the third person and the other in the second. It seems to me that this formulation sends us a very powerful message.

Let us remember who is reciting these *berachos.* It is a newly resurrected person who has only now undergone the ablutions mandated by the use of *negel wasser* in preparation for beginning his divine "service" as he faces the problems that this new day will place in his path. He can use a little guidance as he struggles to define his identity to himself. He is made up of two elements, the physical and the spiritual, which ideally would blend into a perfectly balanced whole, but which, more often than we would want, appear to be in conflict with each other. With which of the two would he identify?

Here is a quote from Rav Dessler (*Michtav MeiEliyahu* II, page 138) as he discusses what happened to Adam HaRishon after he ate from the tree that had been forbidden to him.

> Now, that Adam had sinned, he experienced his evil in-clination in the first person: "*I* want," "*I* desire." However, his better instincts speak to him in the second person, "*You* have this obligation." "*You* are forbidden to do this." We have a situation in which our intellect and our con-science demand that we act in accordance with that which is right, but we experience ourselves as being identified with our base desires. [It is *I* who wants; it is *you* (mind and conscience) who are trying to stop me.] This was not the case with Adam HaRishon before he trespassed into forbidden territory.

The hint that the wording of the two *berachos* sends to our freshly minted *oved* (servant of HaShem) is clear enough. View your physical self from the outside (third person). Take an academic interest in its well-being but do not identify with it. The "I" of your personality should reside with your *neshamah*.

Our second problem, the one that noted that *Asher Yotzar* switches in the middle from third person (*Who fashioned man and created him*) to second person (*It is obvious and known to You*) is more complex. Why was this done and what are we to learn from it?

Actually, we are approaching this question from the wrong angle. We are wondering why a particular style was chosen. But, before we can hope for an answer to that question, we should be asking ourselves what this *berachah* is saying. We will expect the style to suit the message. What is the message?

Let us examine the main body* of the *berachah* for content. It seems to me that it consists of two statements.

1. Great wisdom was involved in forming man as indicated by the many openings and cavities in the body.** (Third person)
2. God is aware of the vulnerability that follows as a result of this complexity. There is much that can go very, very wrong since even a minor malfunction can easily be lethal. (Second person)

If the *berachah* had ended with #1, it would have been a form with which we are familiar from the bulk of the many *berachos* that we say daily. When we eat an apple we praise God for having created it (*Who has created the fruit of the trees*), when we take care of our body's needs, we praise God for having formed it (*Who has formed man*). The fact that we add a description of the body's complexity is not in any way an irregularity. We need only think of the last of the *sheva berachos* to confirm that. If that *berachah* had simply read *Who created joy and gladness*, it would have been a perfectly respectable *berachah*. Nevertheless, we all feel the rightness of the elaboration that follows; it fits and enhances the occasion. *Asher Yotzar* is no different.

That, however, is not the case with #2. I become more and more puzzled as I sit here staring at this passage on my screen. How can a statement that God is aware of our vulnerabilities have a function that makes it a legitimate part of a *berachah*?

---

* By "main body" I mean the text minus the opening formula (*Baruch atah...*until *Asher Yotzar*) and the closing formula (*Baruch Atah HaShem rofeh* till the end).

** Orech Chaim 6:1 offers three possibilities concerning what precisely it is that requires this profound wisdom. For simplicity's sake we will go with first of these three, *That the sheer complexity of the human body, involving as it does many openings (mouth, nostrils and other orifices that lead in and out of the body) and "cavities" (organs such as the lungs, heart, stomach, and brain), points to profound wisdom on the part of the Creator.*

Let us think a little about the concept of vulnerability. Is it good, bad, or indifferent?

I have the feeling that Ramban can help us. First, though, let us read the following passage in Devarim 11:10–12:

> For the land to which you are about to come and possess it—it is not like the Land of Egypt that you left, where you would plant your seed and water it on foot like a vegetable garden.
>
> But the land to which you are about to cross in order to possess it, is a land of hills and valleys. Only from the rain of heaven will you be able to drink water.
>
> It is a land that HaShem your God seeks out, the eyes of HaShem your God are always upon it, from the beginning of the year till the year's end.

Clearly, the Torah is somehow contrasting Eretz Canaan to Egypt. What is the sense of the passage? Rashi, short and sharp as always, makes his idea very clear. On the words, *it is not like Egypt*, he comments, *But it is better*. The rest of the passage is then devoted to demonstrating the advantages that their new home will have over their old.

Ramban has a very different approach.

> The plain meaning of the passage is to take it as a warning....You must be aware that this is not the land of Egypt [where one can always find sufficient water] to irrigate the land from streams and pools as one would do with an herb garden. Do not expect that the land to which you are now about to come will be like that. Rather it is a land of hills and valleys and must rely on rainfall if it is to be watered. It is a thirsty land, requiring abundant rain throughout the year. If you fall short in fulfilling your obligations and the Ribono shel Olam will not send blessed rain, the land will be barren, producing nothing at all.
>
> All this is spelled out in the very next *parshah*, which spells out very clearly that the land will produce its

bounty only as a result of conscientious adherence to the *mitzvos*. Absent that, God will seal the heavens and there will be no rain at all.

For our purposes, verse 12 is the important climax to this passage. Here it is once more: *A land that HaShem your God seeks out, the eyes of HaShem your God are always upon it, from the beginning of the year till the year's end.* Because of its need for rain, God will be a constant presence for the people who will be living there. It transpires that the very vulnerability of the land carries with it the guarantee that the Ribono shel Olam will never be far away. In Egypt, with its guaranteed irrigation system, it was easy to forget the Ribono shel Olam. That can never happen in Eretz Yisrael.

I believe that this Ramban provides the key for understanding the text of the main body of *Asher Yotzar*. Man is a hugely complex mechanism, and it is that complexity that gives us the impetus to laud His wisdom in the first section of the *berachah*. However, it also makes for an uncomfortable vulnerability. So we need the Ribono shel Olam all the time and we need Him close by. If thirsty Eretz Yisrael is the best place for us to be *because* it is thirsty, the accident-prone body makes for an ongoing relationship with the Ribono shel Olam *because* it is constantly at risk.[4]

The choice of the second person in which to couch this second half of the *berachah* is now also readily understandable. Fear of death and of course the hope that it might be avoided or delayed can express itself best in the intimacy of a face-to-face entreaty. Under such circumstances appropriate formality takes a backseat.[5]

At the very moment at which we are engaged in actions of the crassest physicality, the Ribono shel Olam is still very much there in our consciousness. *Asher Yotzar* fits perfectly into the drama of the early morning that we have described in this chapter.

3.

Elokai, Neshamah

My God!
The soul You placed in me is pure.
You created it; You fashioned it; You breathed it into me.
You safeguard it within me
And eventually You will take it from me and
restore it to me in Time to Come.
As long as the soul is within me I gratefully thank You
HaShem, my God and God of my forefathers,
Master of all works, Lord of all souls.
Blessed are You HaShem
Who restores souls to dead bodies. *

*L*et us recall that in the introductory remarks to the previous chapter, we mentioned that our contemplation of *Asher Yotzar* and *Elokai, Neshamah* will rest on the opinion of the Vilna Ga'on, namely, that these two *berachos* belong together. They form a twosome because, as we celebrate our "rebirth" every morning,** we thank the Ribono shel Olam for both our physical and our spiritual integrity.

All the more, then, we are (or should be) shocked by the sudden switch from a neutral third-person structure (*Who*

---

* This translation is lifted straight from the ArtScroll Siddur, of course with permission. I reproduce it as is because many of you will be familiar with it. In the course of this chapter I will be suggesting significant changes in some of the renderings.

** Please reread the introductory remarks to the previous chapter. As we think about *Elokai, Neshamah*, you will want to reenter the world of the Rashba—delineated there—who views our awakening each morning as a form of rebirth. The chapter that you are about to begin is written with an awareness of the Rashba, in the form of his ideas, hovering in the background.

has created man) to the intensely individualistic mood expressed in *Elokai, Neshamah* by the constant use of the first person (as evidenced by expressions such as *my God, in me, with me, for me*).* In our analysis we will try to penetrate to the mood of this passage in search of a reason for this change of perspective.

Elokai, Neshamah has a throbbing, staccato sound. Its many short salvos pound our sensibilities with strong, economically phrased, and therefore powerfully aimed blasts of reality that, we suddenly realize, we would ignore at our peril. We will split up *Elokai, Neshamah* into its natural divisions and think about each one on its own. After we have dealt separately with these small chunks, each packed tight with implications of the highest order, we will attempt a statement on its cumulative message.

MY GOD: It seems to me that this is a quasi-formulaic wording at the opening of a prayer that seeks to strike a tone of intimacy and personal connection. I am thinking particularly of the so-called entreaties (*tachanunim*)** that it is customary to say at the end of *Shemoneh Esrei*. Berachos 16b and 17a teach that after we have completed our *Shemoneh Esrei*, we have an opportunity to ad-lib our own prayers.*** The Gemara provides a long list of personal petitions to illustrate how different people took advantage of this dispensation. Of the many examples listed, only two couched this voluntary prayer in the first-person singular. These two, and none other, opened their supplication with the word *Elokai*. It seems to be as I sur-

---

* The explanation that we offered in the previous chapter for the internal switch within *Asher Yotzar* would not apply here.

The conclusion of the *berachah* (*Who restores souls...*), interestingly enough, reverts to the third person. We shall get back to this issue further along in this chapter.

** Represented for us by *Elokai, Netzor* with which we customarily close our *Shemoneh Esrei*.

*** The *Mishnah Berurah* cites *Chayei Adam*: "It is correct and fitting that every person pray each day for his needs and livelihood and that Torah not depart from the lips of his children and grandchildren and that his children be servants of HaShem and that there not be found any deficiency in his children."

mised. When you want intimacy with the Ribono shel Olam, that is how you begin.

THE SOUL THAT YOU GAVE TO ME IS PURE: Please join me in my attempt to come to grips with this very difficult *berachah*. Let us look at it with fresh eyes. Let us wipe our memories clean and pretend to ourselves that we have never seen or said it before.

Okay. Ready?

Let us read it from beginning to end. Slowly now, very carefully, very thoughtfully, even hungrily, in the sense that we are eager not to lose a single crumb from the feast that is spread before us. Let us hear its music and absorb its rhythms. Let us, above all, find delight in its message.

What message?

Here you have my problem. I find it extremely difficult to pin down a single coherent theme.

Let us try this. Let us remove the following words: *is pure* and *all the time that the soul is within me....Master of all souls.)* and the problem disappears. The subject is the wondrous partnership between body and soul. *Elokai, Neshamah* is indeed a straight and logical continuation from *Asher Yotzar*. In that *berachah* we acknowledged God's wisdom in fashioning our bodies and, with the words *u'mafli la'asos*, opened the door to a contemplation of the miracle of the purely spiritual *neshamah* residing in the purely physical body. We then move on to *Elokai, Neshamah* in order to fill in the details of that "unearthly" combination. The entire *berachah* (after our excisions) is devoted to a listing of those details, up to and including the return of that soul to that body after death.

Everything is as it should be.

In what way does the statement that the *neshamah* is *pure* belong in this context? And what role does our assertion that we *gratefully thank* the Ribono shel Olam play?

I have some suggestions to make. Let us test the extent to which they resonate with you.

It all begins with what superficially would appear to be a contradiction in the Maharal.

Niddah 30b teaches that before a child is born, he is made to swear some oaths whereby he obliges himself to accept certain undertakings. "Know that HaShem is pure and His servants are pure and the soul He put in you is pure. If you guard it in purity, good. If not, it will be taken from you."

Maharal, in the *Chidushei Aggada* explains:

One should not think that, having been placed into a physical body, the soul loses its holiness. That is not the case. It does not lose its holiness even though it is inside a human body. This is so because…it retains its own identity and does not blend into the body. Therefore, before we are born it is impressed upon us that as HaShem is pure and His servants are pure, we are to guard our soul in purity.*

The gist of Maharal's remarks is as follows. It may certainly be assumed that the *neshamah*, coming, as it does, from the world of the Ribono shel Olam and His ministrants, would be pure. However, there is every reason to wonder whether that purity can be maintained after it enters the body, which, of course, belongs in the world of physicality and uncleanliness. The potential human is informed that that is not the case. As Maharal explains, the *neshamah* does not become a "citizen" in the body's world: "it does not blend."

In chapter 28 of *Gevuros HaShem*, Maharal offers certain ideas that might be thought to be in contradiction to his Niddah remarks. There, he discusses the Chazal that while we are in our mother's womb, each of us is taught the entire Torah. Once we are born, however, an angel comes and hits us on the mouth, at which point we forget it all. We do not need to quote the entire piece. Suffice to say that Maharal had made the point that speech, involving as it does the movement of the mouth and lips, can be viewed as a symbol of physicality. He continues:

---

* This is a paraphrase.

When we understand this, we can also understand what our Sages say in the Gemara (Niddah 30b). When a child is born, an angel comes and taps him on his mouth and that makes the infant forget the entire Torah. Why is the knock specifically on the mouth? For the mouth is the place from which a person receives life (a breath of life is breathed into a physical shell and this makes a man). This physicality causes us to forget the Torah....When the soul is not connected to the physical (before birth), the soul is separate, detached, and completely intellectual (*sichlis*); it can know the entire Torah. But when we are born...the soul attaches to the physical, the person lives, and his very physical existence makes him forget the Torah, for he is no longer pure intellect.*

The gist of Maharal's explanation is that the fetus's ability to absorb the Torah lies in the fact that within the womb he is removed from the outer, physical world and has the characteristics of a purely spiritual being. Once born, however, he is *joined* to the physical body and the Torah, dependent as it is at this point on pure spirituality, leaves him.

The apparent contradiction is clear enough. In the Niddah passage we learn that the *neshamah* is *nivdal* (separate) from the body and retains its purity, while in *Gevuros HaShem* we learn that it is joined to the body and therefore loses its affinity to Torah.

The problem is clear and, as far as I can see, allows of only one answer. The *neshamah* is indeed joined to the body and *nevertheless* the state of purity is not touched by this proximity. *Relative* to purity, the *neshamah* remains unattached.

This assertion opens up the possibility of an entirely new meaning for our phrase, and onward, for the entire *berachah*. It is to be translated as follows:

---

* This, too, is partly a paraphrase.

The *neshamah* that You attached to my physical being [thereby making its affinity to Torah impossible] *nevertheless* remains pure.

Taken thus, the following three statements: *You created it...fashioned it...blew it into me...*(see below for a more precise examination of the respective meanings) would also take on a new meaning. Instead of being simple statements of fact, they are offered as justifications of the earlier statement. The Ribono shel Olam (for reasons that we will understand a little better further along) decided that the piece of Godliness that we know as the *neshamah* should remain *pure* although it is lodged in a physical body. In order to facilitate this, He specifically "created" and "formed" it so that He would be able to "breathe" it into us in such a way that it will retain its separate personality even though, relative to other matters, it has blended into one with the body.

The need to stress the fact that the *neshamah* retains its purity will become clear when we get to the section beginning, *as long as the neshamah is within me.*

YOU CREATED IT, YOU FASHIONED IT. Things are getting really exciting here. We know from Ramban to Bereishis 1:1 that ב ר א (*b-r-h*) used here for creation is used only for a coming into existence *ex nihilo*, existence *growing out of nothingness*. For forming an existing "something" into an appropriate "shape," the term י צ ר (*y-tz-r*) is appropriate. The wording here implies that the *neshamah* was first "made" out of "nothing"* and then "shaped" in a way that made it fitting for just me (*bi*).**

---

* I have put the words *something* and *nothing* into quotes since, in the context of a *neshamah*, they can mean nothing at all to us.

** When does this act of creation take place? From the simple text, one would have supposed that it is done for each individual as his time comes to be born. I have checked siddur commentaries that are available to me and came across certain ambiguities. The *Eitz Yosef* (printed in the *Otzar HaTefillos*) is the only one among the commentators that I saw who says expressly that this creation took place together with the Creation of the rest of the world.

The implications are, of course, shattering. Each one of us is hit every single morning with the, to us, absolutely outlandish idea that in order to place each of us* in this world of ours, the Ribono shel Olam had to reach into the void of primeval nothingness and engage in an act of creation that was on a par with the bringing into being of the entire cosmos!**

YOU BREATHED IT INTO ME. In Hebrew: אתה נפחתה בי, *atah nafachta bi:* The expression is derived from Bereishis 2:7, *He breathed a living soul into his nostrils.* Great Torah scholars who have reached the point at which they understand something of the Torah's secrets will certainly want to think of the Zohar's statement that, *When we breathe out we are expelling something of our own being.*

YOU GUARD IT WITHIN ME. What exactly does this phrase convey?

How does the *neshamah* feel about being lodged inside a human being? When the time comes for its host to die, does the *neshamah* leave with a sigh of relief, or is it a sad parting? There is a beautiful passage in Devarim Rabba 11:10 that describes how the *neshamah* of Moshe Rabbeinu reacted when the Ribono shel Olam announced that the time had come for him to leave this world:

> [Moshe's] soul protests: I know that...it was You Who breathed me into in the body of Moshe. I have been there for 120 years. So I know. Is there a body in the world purer than the body of Moshe, which was never exposed to anything ugly? I love it and I don't want to leave it.

I do not think that this issue impacts seriously upon the thesis that I want to propound in this chapter.

* "Each of us," with all our imperfections. "Each of us" in all our depressing insignificance. Makes you think, does it not? I have the feeling that a little more concentration and thought in our *davening* could put half the psychiatrists in the world out of business.

** *In the beginning God "created" (b-r-h) heaven and earth.*

HaShem responds: You will lose nothing by leaving! Your place will be among the holiest of the holy.

The soul argues: "Angels, too, can sometimes fall short of their standards. Not Moshe! From the day You revealed Yourself to him in the burning bush, he had no relations with his wife...I plead with You to leave me in the body of Moshe."

At that moment, HaShem took Moshe's soul with a kiss planted on his mouth.*

The implication is certainly that at the death of people other than Moshe Rabbeinu, there would have been fewer problems. The *neshamah* would have been less comfortable in those bodies and would have willingly returned to its normal environment. It is time to reacquaint ourselves with the famous passage in *Mesilas Yesharim* 1:

The soul will never feel satisfied (Koheles 6:7). Think of a princess married to a country yokel. No gift of his will ever please her. She is, after all, royalty, reared on the luxuries of the palace.

So it is with the soul. Nothing that our physical world can offer will ever mean anything to her. Down here she feels out of her element.

Perhaps that is the reason why it is necessary for the Ribono shel Olam to guard our souls in our bodies. On their own they might well be bent on escape.

IN THE FUTURE YOU WILL TAKE IT...AND RETURN IT. Please see the previous passages. Their thrust is to stress that the marriage of our *neshamos* to our bodies is absolute and permanent. Together they form a unique identity that is to last forever.

But there will be a break. At death we will have to part. Of that period in our history we know nothing at all. For us, it is

* Paraphrase.

shrouded in mystery. For us it is important only to know that the split will not affect our compound identity. Our souls will depart—they will also return. The identity that was crafted when we were originally combined will outlive that trauma. In God's good time we will come together once more.

At this point we come up against a difficult conundrum. The identity between body and soul seems to be so absolute that it can withstand a break of millennia. People who died thousands of years ago will still be reunited with their souls. But does that not seem to militate against the idea that we worked out earlier, that as far as the soul's purity is concerned it maintains an entirely *separate* personality? How can this be? Read on! It appears that God has His reasons.

ALL THE TIME THE BODY IS WITHIN ME, I THANK YOU. We need to visit Berachos 10a. The Gemara establishes that there are five criteria that will determine who is fit to pronounce God's praises. God is understood to have five significant qualities. 1.) He fills the entire world. 2.) He can see although He cannot be seen. 3.) He sustains the entire world. 4.) He is pure. 5.) He occupies the inner chambers. Our soul, since it, too, shares in these five qualities, is therefore qualified to praise the Ribono shel Olam.

This *sugia* obviously deals with esoteric matters that cannot mean anything to us. We will not expect to understand in any meaningful way what is being said. As we develop this section we will discover that, in the present context, only the fourth faculty, God's purity, is of interest to us.

Still we have to do some technical housekeeping. The Gemara's source for assuming specifically five categories is the fact that between Tehilim 103 and 104 we have the phrase ברכי נפשי את ה', *Bless HaShem, O my soul*, repeated five times.

But what does "blessing" have to do with "praising"? The answer is short and sharp. Radak teaches that, in fact, they have nothing to do with each other, and the translation that we just used is incorrect. The root *b-r-ch* really means "to increase." A blessing is a prayer that the recipient of that blessing be increased in whatever context the *berachah* is being given.

That is not a concept that can be applied to the Ribono shel Olam, the "all-perfect" Being. We therefore cannot "bless" Him. When humans utter a *berachah* to God, they are not blessing Him. They are "singing His praises." The translation of ברכי נפשי את ה' is *not* "Bless HaShem O my soul" but "Sing praises to HaShem O my soul."*

Earlier in this chapter we asked how the statement that the *neshamah* is pure fits into the current context. What does this particular faculty contribute to what we had thought was the general theme? We have reached a point at which we are going to be able to suggest an answer. That answer will involve a complete turnabout on the subject of what, in fact, this *berachah* is all about.

I will argue that the *berachah's* theme is the expression of our determination to turn our very lives into a song of glory to the Ribono shel Olam. The two segments* that, earlier in this chapter we had thought to be unconnected to anything that the rest of the *nusach* was saying are, to the contrary, the life and soul of the *berachah*; they stand at its very center while what we had thought to be the real theme is, in actuality, only commentary.

The main part of the *berachah* reads as follows:

אלקי נשמה שנתת בי טהורה היא
God, the soul you put within me is pure.

[and therefore none of the five necessary faculties that the soul has in common with the Ribono shel Olam are missing. We recall that purity is one of the five categories.

This is possible although this soul is, in certain ways, joined to my physical body because:]

אתה בראתה, אתה יצרתה ואתה נפחתה בי
You created it, You fashioned it, and You placed it within me.

[You custom-designed it so that in spite of being joined
to the body, it should retain its purity.]

And moreover:

ואתה משמרה בקרבי
You safeguard it in me,

ואתה עתיד לטלה ממני ולהחזירה בי לעתיד לבוא
*And in the future, You will take it from me, and
in the future to come You will return it to me.*

[You made it a permanent part of my personality by en-
suring that it would not be able to escape and by guaran-
teeing that even after my death it will still be tied to me
because it is destined to be returned to me.

So, it turns out that this is who I am. I am a pure soul,
joined, it is true, to a physical body, but, nonetheless for
that, maintaining my primeval purity. When Dovid
HaMelech exhorted me (ברכי נפשי) to sing God's praises,
he knew what he was doing. Being pure and therefore
equipped with all the necessary five faculties, I am indeed worthy of singing songs of glory to the Ribono shel
Olam.

And, therefore:]

כל זמן שהנשמה בקרבי מודה אני לפניך...
All the time the soul is in me, I will praise You.*

[I will make sure that every moment of my life will constitute a song of glory to You.]

The need to stress that the *neshamah* is *pure* is now, of
course, obvious. Four out of the five faculties enumerated

---

* Please turn back to endnote 1 in the second chapter of this book. There we
demonstrate in detail that the root י ד ה means not only "to thank" but also
"to praise." Just as *Elokai, Neshamah* begins with an exhortation to praise (see
above), so it ends with the assertion that this is precisely what I intend to do
with my life.

by the Gemara are obviously present without any problems. Our souls obviously fill the whole body, are hidden in the innermost parts of our beings, and so on. The only one of the five that needed defending is the *purity* requirement. We might have supposed that this standard would be impossible to maintain. We therefore declare proudly from the very beginning that there are no problems. God planned ahead and made sure that nothing required for living the life that He would want us to live will be missing!

MASTER OF ALL WORKS, LORD OF ALL SOULS. What do these two titles, particularly when spliced together, convey? It is not a combination that occurs frequently. In the *nusach Ashkenaz* in which I *daven*, I think it is unique to *Elokai, Neshamah*, while the *nusach Sefard* has it also in *Yishtabach*.

I believe that, as I have explained our *berachah*, the meaning lies ready at hand. The central idea that our *berachah* postulates is really counterintuitive.

We would certainly have supposed that once infused into the body, our souls would have lost their purity. Before we leave the *berachah*, we would certainly appreciate an explanation.

Here we have it.

The Ribono shel Olam is addressed in *this berachah*, and at least in *nusach Ashkenaz* as Master of all works, *Ribon kol hama'asim* and Lord of all souls, *Adon kol haneshamos*. The word מעשה is of course formed from the *shoresh* ע ש ה (*a-s-ah*), which is used to describe the action of creation: ויכל אלקים ביום השביעי את כל מלאכתו אשר **עשה** (*The Lord ceased, on the seventh day, all the work He had made*). Accordingly *Ribon kol hama'asim* connotes the Master of the whole created, physical world. *Adon kol haneshamos* is self-explanatory. The two names spliced together provides the answer to the question that left us puzzled above. He Who is Master of all that is physical and all that is pure can work things out thus that the infusion of the *neshamah tehorah* into the body need not corrupt the *neshamah*.

WHO RESTORES SOULS TO DEAD BODIES. This conclusion picks up the phrase ולהחזירה בי (*and will return to me*) from the body of the *berachah*. I suggest that it does so because after the details of HaShem creating, fashioning, and breathing the soul into us, all of which are designed to establish the absolute identity between the pure soul and the physical body, the closing phrase, that upon our death the Ribono shel Olam takes the *neshamah* with the intention of returning it to us at *techiyas hameisim* (*the resurrection of the dead*) is the most telling argument of all. What possible connection can there be between the pure soul and the lifeless body that is all that is left of us after death? And yet, the Ribono shel Olam does just that. The fusion of the identities is absolute. That this final *berachah* is switched to the third person, another of the problems that we left unsolved earlier, is also understandable. This idea that after the passage of millennia the Ribono shel Olam would return the appropriate soul to the appropriate body is so astounding that the familiar second person would be totally out of court.

4.

Oter Yisrael B'sif'arah

*E*very morning as we go to *Shacharis,* we have much work cut out for us; and all this before we ever reach *Baruch SheOmar,* the formal beginning of the morning prayer. Let us spend a little time examining what we are actually supposed to be experiencing at that point in our daily *davening.* We are in for some big surprises.

Let us see whether we can make all this work for us.

For me, and I imagine for you, too, the last three chapters have not been easy going. It is not only that the material is hard—we expect that and relish the challenge. It is that each of the passages that we covered *Modeh Ani, Asher Yotzar,* and *Elokai, Neshamah*—seems fraught with implications of a *Yiddishkeit* that harbors expectations way beyond anything of which we had been aware. Instead of just leaving us with a feeling of fuzzy satisfaction at making it to *Shacharis* more or less on time, these passages hit us with duties that seem, indeed are, very, very demanding.

Still, that is the way things are and it is time for us to be grateful that we are bidden to rise to the occasion.

Here is the relevant *Mishnah Berurah* (4:1): *Our Sages ordained that every morning we are called upon to enter into a state of sanctity by washing our hands from a vessel, precisely as did the kohanim who washed their hands from the* kiyor (the basin placed in the Temple courtyard from which the ablutions were made) *before they began their daily divine service.* So, all of a sudden we are "*kohanim*" with a day of divine service stretching out before us. We may be driving a bus through town, we may be pumping gas or sweeping streets, but we need to go through a formal ablution before we get to work.*

Well, it is time to recall that in an earlier chapter we found out the extent to which our seemingly innocent little *Modeh Ani* is freighted with some very heavy entailments.

The same was, of course, true of *Asher Yotzar*, and *Elokai, Neshamah*. You probably recall how, in *Asher Yotzar* we discovered an edifying, but at the same time rather terrifying, proximity to the Ribono shel Olam. In *Elokai, Neshamah* we were brought face-to-face with the expectation that our lives are to be lived as rendering a song of praise to Him.

All in all, we can hardly be blamed if already at this very early stage of *Shacharis*, we conclude that, *Ez iz schwer tzu zein a Yid!* ("It is difficult to be a Jew!")** Being Jewish—living Jewish—is not easy! However, as we shall learn through-

---

* Clearly the use of "*kohanim*" and "divine service" in this context is not to be taken literally. Commentators point out that we wash only our hands, not our feet as was obligatory in the Beis HaMikdash. Our washing is a symbolic gesture, no more. Still it may not be taken lightly. Chazal, who ordained these ablutions, were deadly serious in regard to the ramifications of this ordinance. It has many halachic implications. What we have learned in the last three chapters and will continue to develop in this one clearly stands at the very center of Jewish living.

While I have not seen the following in any particular source, my intuition tells me that it is nevertheless true. Once Chazal determined that, at the start of the day, we would do well to view ourselves as "*kohanim*" beginning our daily "divine service," it seems logical that they expected us to draw necessary conclusions. If, for example, our *negel wasser* cup stands in for the *kiyor*, it seems reasonable to assume that our work place would, at the very least, approximate the Temple courtyard. The rule in the real Temple courtyard required that the *kohanim* never sit down; that they be constantly poised for service (Yoma 25a). There was to be no dawdling. Of course, since, to the best of my knowledge, no currently applicable *halachos* are drawn from this rule, it would be up to each one of us to work out for himself the degree to which this thinking would obligate him.

** One of the great Chasidic masters is reputed to have said, "It is true that sometimes it feels hard to be a Jew. But, believe me, it is a lot harder not to be one."

out this book, it is very, very rewarding. Just substitute *"gut"* (good) for *"schwer"* (difficult) and you will be on the doorstep of some very profound insights. *Ez is gut tzu zein a Yid!* A serious commitment to serious *Yiddishkeit*—really living Jewish—is great!

We are now ready to move on to the *berachah, Oter Yisrael BeSif'arah*, the *berachah* that asserts that God crowns us with glory.

* * *

Once we finish with the first set of *berachos,* those with which we have dealt in the past few chapters, we move on to a different series, those *berachos* with which we thank God for providing us with the conditions that we require for living a full and satisfying life.* The first of these deals with the gift of sight, the second asserts that God *clothes the naked* and so on. The final two *berachos* in this list** read, "He girds Israel with strength" and "He crowns Israel with Glory." Many commentators note that, whereas in the other *berachos* we thank the Ribono shel Olam in general terms—God grants sight to *everybody,* clothes *all* the naked, frees *all* those who are shackled, and so on—in these two final *berachos* we thank Him for girding and crowning specifically *Yisrael.* Why should this be so? Commentators that are available to me all offer more or less the same answer, which I quote here in the words of the *Mishnah Berurah* 46:9.

> Israel is mentioned in these two *berachos* but not in any of the others. Here is the explanation: All the earlier *berachos* speak to universal needs. Everyone needs to be able to see and so on. However, the belt and the head-covering of which these two *berachos* speak are

---

* The three earlier "Who has not made me..." *berachos* stand on their own and have no connection to the grouping with which we are about to deal. The former have their source in Menachos 43b, the latter in Berachos 60b.

** Actually these two are followed by another one, *HaNosein LaYa'ef Ko'ach,* Who grants strength to the weak. However, I have described the two that precede this one as the final ones in the list, since this last one was a later addition. The others are all mentioned in the Gemara; this one is not.

specifically Jewish concerns. The belt has the function of making a division between the upper and lower parts of the body. This is viewed as appropriate when we stand before God in prayer. The head covering derives its significance from Shabbos 154 where we are exhorted: "Cover your head so that, by doing this, you express the awe in which you face your Master."

It seems to me that if we are considering the relationship between these two *berachos* and the others, there is more than just the mention of *"Yisrael"* that makes them stand out. While the others deal with actual, physical facts on the ground, God gifts us with sight, with clothing, with terra firma under our feet and so on, these latter two speak of a more profound dimension. They do not simply thank the Ribono shel Olam for giving us belts and hats. Both these would have been included under, *Who clothes the naked.* They speak of *might* and *glory,* not of haberdashery. I would argue that the use of *Yisrael* in these two *berachos* derives from the fact that they inhabit a world all of their own.

How so?

THE WORLD OF THE LAST TWO BERACHOS

Let us begin with the observation that a movement within a given series, from the universal to the particular, let us say from the human or even from the animal world to the specifically Jewish, would not be unique to the *Birkos HaShachar,* the morning *berachos.* You may have noticed that this is precisely what we do in *Birkas HaMazon.* The first *berachah* is all-inclusive with never a hint that Jews might be different from the gentiles or even from the animals. The second *berachah* then works its way through thanking God for our land, our covenant with Him and for the Torah that was His gift to us. From there, in the third *berachah,* we move on to Yerushalayim and the Beis HaMikdash.

So we need not be surprised to find the final two *berachos* of the *Birkos HaShachar* breaking the mold in which the earlier *berachos* had been fashioned. Those had thanked the Ribono shel Olam for making life—for the whole of humanity—livable in the wonderful, physical world that He had so lovingly created. That accomplished, the *berachos* turn to a different matter. In our vast universe in which everything is interlocked and interdependent, there is a stranger, a pesky misfit who does not play by the rules. His name is *Yisrael!** He is a fighter—and a winner (remember Yaakov and the angel). He uses superhuman tenacity (*gevurah*) to get where he needs to get, and his victories crown him with glory (*tif'arah*). *Birkos HaShachar* must accommodate him, too, and does so with the two *berachos* that we are discussing.

Here is my thesis: The two *berachos* that we are discussing, but particularly *Oter Yisrael BeSif'arah*, which actually brings the series to a close, are the lookout platform on the top of the mountain. *Negel wasser* as we learned to appreciate it, *Modeh Ani* as we understood its stupendous message, *Asher Yotzar* and *Elokai, Neshamah*, which, together, lift the bar that we all are expected to vault to dazzling heights, all these are the way stations that lead onward and upward as we make our slow and difficult path to the top.

We washed our hands in our personal *kiyor*. We became "*kohanim*" of sorts, each one of us embarking upon the personal divine service that the Ribono shel Olam assigned to us. We are aware of God's breathtaking proximity (*Asher Yotzar*) and of the song that He would have us sing (*Elokai, Neshamah*). We are ready for the climax. The head coverings that we put on just after we get out of bed are our priestly vestments, they define us in our Jewishness, they reflect our honor and our glory!

This last sentence needs a little elaboration. We will take care of that now, and then we will have brought the long and complex "drama" with which we have dealt in these past four chapters to a close.

* * *

* We recall how the Kuzari expands the four basic groupings: inanimate, animate, living, and speaking into five, with Israel providing the fifth category.

We have argued that the belt and the head covering that are, respectively, the subject of the two *berachos* with which we are dealing can be viewed as the priestly vestments, the honor and glory of the *kehunah*, the state of being a *kohen*, to which every Jew aspires as he gets ready to launch into the body of our morning prayers.

Is there any logic to the selection of just these two from among the four garments that made up the vestments of the ordinary *kohanim*?

There is. Here is the background.

One of the duties that the *kohanim* performed in the Beis HaMikdash was the removal of the accumulated ashes from the altar. This was a messy business and the Torah hints that, while doing what needed to be done, the *kohanim* who were privileged to perform this vital task would wear clothes that were inferior in quality to their regular vestments. In Yoma 23b we have a disagreement between Reish Lakish and R. Yochanan concerning the number of formal vestments they would wear during that activity. Reish Lakish, based on VaYikra 6:3, is of the opinion that they wore only two of the four that they would normally wear for other duties: the trousers and the shirt. R. Yochanan asserts that they wore all the four.

R. Meir Simchah of Dvinsk, the Meshech Chochmah, offers an ingenious explanation for Reish Lakish's opinion that only the shirt and trousers were worn for this activity. Here is a quote:

> "For the sons of Aaron you shall make tunics and make them sashes; and you shall make them headdresses for glory and splendor."* It is very possible that this verse serves as the basis of Reish Lakish's opinion that the regular head-covering and the belt were not worn for this activity. Our verse makes clear that these two (though not the two others) were marks of "honor" and "splendor." As such, they were clearly not suitable for this par-

---

* I borrowed this translation from the ArtScroll TaNaCh.

ticular service concerning which we know that inferior clothes were to be worn.

The two *berachos* with which we are dealing are indeed a fitting finale to the *Birkos HaShachar*. We all know that most of us are not really *kohanim* and that those of us who are, are nevertheless, during our *galus* experience, unable to function as we once did and will in God's good time once more in the future.

Still, from the moment that we wake up in the morning and reach for our *negel wasser,* we indulge ourselves in a benign fiction that really is no fiction at all. As have most other words in our precious "Torah" language, the word *"kohen"* too has a wide range of application and meaning. In his heart of hearts, the simplest Jew knows that if he is not a halachic *kohen,* he is still a *"kohen."* The *negel wasser* cup that he used this morning was his *kiyor,* his workplace is his Temple courtyard, and his struggles with life in whatever context they play themselves out are his divine service. He knows, or ought to know, he feels, or ought to feel, that when he puts on his head covering, whether a *rosh yeshivah's* hat, a rebbe's *shtraimel,* or the baseball cap that he wears then, on his menial job, he is being bathed in glory.

Our duty is clear. Let us be sure to know what we ought to know, to feel what we ought to feel.

Oh God!
Let my baseball cap
Turn out to be
A crown of glory.
I am a member in good standing
of the "Kingdom of Kohanim"
that the Ribono Shel Olam envisioned
as we all stood together at Sinai.
Oh God! It is so good to be a yid!
Thank you.

PART II

Birkas HaMazon

5.

The Three Berachos

Is there anything in this world more suggestive of power than a lion's roar? It is aggressive, assertive, and bellicose. "This is my territory; do not encroach!" "These are my females; do not dare to challenge me for them!" Above all it is loud. Biologists claim that it carries up to five miles across the tundra.

But the truth is that it travels much, much farther than that. They hear it up there in the heavens:

> *You bring on darkness and it is night;*
> *when all the beasts of the forest stir.*
> *The lions roar for prey,*
> *seeking their food from God.*
> (Tehilim 104:20–21)

But, you know what? Up there it sounds quite different. By the time it reaches the world of truth, the roar of self-assertion sounds much more like a whimper of vulnerability. The roar speaks of needs: "My God, I am so scared. Is my hegemony in this territory secure? Can I be sure that by tomorrow I will not have been driven from my pride,* displaced by rivals that even now may be lurking in the darkness?" Above all, "Oh God, I am hungry. My heavy mane gets in the way of my being an effective hunter. Hunger hurts! My God, where will I turn? What will become of me?"

That last cry galvanizes the heavenly hordes into action. Somewhere, not too far away, a herd of wildebeest is quietly

---

* A "pride" is for lions what a "school" is for fish. Both terms are used to describe a group that in one way or another belongs together.

grazing. Suddenly—who knows how or why?—an instinct is triggered. "Run!" They gallop off along a path that had already, somehow, been anticipated by the females of the pride. At the right moment, in a perfect symphony of movement, an unerring leap, a slashing claw, a snapping, crunching jaw, and a straggler is taken. The females, the actual hunters, fall upon the prey that seems rightly to be theirs. It does not take long for them to be disillusioned. The male who has taken no active part in the kill soon ambles up and begins his leisurely meal. He, too, is one of God's creatures and, deserving or not, God cares for every single one of them.

HE PROVIDES FOOD FOR ALL FLESH
FOR HIS KINDNESS
KNOWS NO BOUNDS.

* * *

What about us? The lion eats and we eat. In physical terms we are very much first cousins. Is there a difference in what happens? Are we, in this area of our lives, simply human lions?

Enter the life-altering, profoundly moving, artfully constructed *Birkas HaMazon*. Once we have really, really decided to enter its thought-world instead of simply mumbling a boring formula, nothing need ever be the same. Sounds strange, does it not? We have all *bentched* for years, have as children earned countless cookies for "*bentching* nicely," and nothing in us has really changed. Why does its magic not work for us? Here is why. As children we learned it by rote; as adults we repeat it by rote. The system practically guarantees that we will go through life as really no more than youngsters wearing grown-up clothes. Purim is great, but not for every day in the year!

Let us emancipate ourselves from our childhood. It is told of some of the Chasidic masters that they would immerse themselves in a *mikveh* before they sat down to eat, the same gesture precisely that they undertook before their prayers. The one experience was, for them, as fraught with sanctity as was the other. What did they know that we do not know?

Read on, because we are about to learn their secret.

Take a look at the first of the four *berachos* that *Birkas*

HaMazon comprises. Is it not strange? We humans are lumped together with the "lions" of this world. The entire wording of the *berachah* bids us confront ourselves as no more than one creature among the myriads upon which God lavishes His care. He feeds "the entire world," He gives food "to all flesh." Finally, He "sustains them all." No differentiation there at all. This blessing does not do much for our egos, does it? But, once more, read on!

I venture to claim that the second *berachah* of *Birkas HaMazon* is the equivalent of a year's worth of *mussar shmuessen*—if we read it right. For this stupendous *berachah* we are going to do some close reading.

The second *berachah* of *Birkas HaMazon* is where we break free of the pack that claimed us among its own during the first *berachah*. It is true that we ingest food, just as do all the other creatures of this, our physical world, but that is where the similarity stops. It is only *klal Yisrael*, equipped, as we shall see, with *bris*, *Eretz*, and Torah, the foundational elements of our peoplehood, for whom the food that we eat contributes to a truly "living"* life. A beautiful land, emancipation from slavery, God's mark upon our bodies, and His Torah in our minds and hearts together define who and what we are.

Let us see how all this works out.

HASHEM, OUR GOD, WE THANK YOU. Who is "we" and why do we thank HaShem?** After what we have learned in the past few paragraphs, we know the answer. "We," *klal Yisrael*, are asserting our uniqueness and thanking the Ribono shel Olam for it. *Birkas HaMazon*, as we shall learn as we go along, is an exercise in appreciating God's gifts at an ever-rising level of experience, and this second *berachah* is the first rung on the ladder. We do indeed have much for which we can be very, very grateful.

---

* For this, see below on the words *and for the life, grace, and loving-kindness.*

** Remember that the root letters ה ד י (*y-d-ah*) with the preposition על (על שהנחלת לאבותינו...), always means *to thank*. See Chapter 1.

AND BECAUSE YOU GAVE OUR FOREFATHERS A DE-
SIRABLE, GOOD, AND SPACIOUS LAND AS A HERITAGE.
I sense a little awkwardness in the fact that the list of gifts
concerning which we are to express our gratitude should
begin with the physical beauty of the land. It is followed by
1.) our release from Egypt, 2.) our redemption from slavery,
3.) the mitzvah of *bris milah*, and 4.) the Torah. Even before we
try to understand in what sense each of these four makes the
cut, I suspect that we would intuitively define each of them as
matters of the spirit. Do they belong in a list that begins with
Eretz Yisrael's beauty? Is there some disjunction here?

I do not think so. The Torah's views on physical beauty are
not our direct concern in this chapter,* but a brief survey is
nevertheless appropriate. We might begin with Nedarim 20b
where we learn:

> They asked Aima Shalom, "Why are your children so
> unusually good looking?" She answered, "[My husband]
> does not communicate with me (a euphemism for con-
> jugal intimacy) either in the early evening or the early
> morning [when other women are walking around in the
> street and his thoughts might wander to one of them],
> but only at midnight [when the streets are empty].
> Moreover [when he approaches me he does so with ex-
> treme *tznius*]."**

I think that it is also appropriate to quote Kesubos 112a:***

---

* I deal with this issue in detail in my book on Yerushalayim, *Harp Strings
and Heart Strings*, in chapter 10, "City of Beauty," and chapter 15, "A Synagogue
Called וַיִּתֵּר שְׁיָּ." Since Chazal teach us that of the ten measures of beauty that
descended upon the world, Yerushalayim took nine, this is a subject that is
right at home there. If you have access to that book and are interested in following this up, I would suggest that you take a peek. Here we will limit ourselves to a couple of short quotes.
** *Harp Strings*, page 70.
*** *Harp Strings*, page 95.

R. Abba used to kiss the stones of Acco. R. Chanina used to repair the roads. [When it was hot] Rav Ami and Rav Asi made sure to move to a shady spot. [When it was cold] they would look for a place warmed by the sun. R. Chiya bar Gamda used to roll around in the dust. Is it not written that, Your servants have adored her very stones, have cherished her dust? (Tehilim 102:15.)

Why was it that just the greatest *rabbanim* and *talmidei chachamim* appreciated Eretz Yisrael's beauty?

It is because they understood the inner being that animated the outer form; they knew that the charm that met their eyes was no more than the physical manifestation of the sanctity that constituted the land's soul. In this matter R. Yehudah HaLevi in his *Kuzari* is going to be our rebbi. Here is what he tells us at 2:62.

The Rabbi said: I have already told you that the Divine Presence was in the midst of the Jewish people like a soul resting within a person's body. It provided them with a Divine life force and a radiance and splendor in their bodies, their clothes, and their dwellings. When It departed from them, their counsel became foolish, their bodies shriveled, and their beauty retreated.*

Things begin to fall into place as follows. The phrase, "for You have given to our forefathers as a heritage a desirable, good, and spacious land," serves as an ideal bridge between the universalism of the first *berachah* and the particularism of the second. This latter one tells us that the overt similarity that we detected earlier—every creature eats—does not mean that there is an absolute congruence among all those living organisms. With the realization that the land that God gave us is not only holy but also beautiful, we have the basis upon

* The translation is taken with permission from Rabbi N. Doniel Korobkin's translation of the *Kuzari*, published by Feldheim. Get it if you can. It is a beautiful piece of work.

which to progress through the various stages of awareness of the significance of our *human,* "soul-intoxicated" physicality. Although surface beauty is usually just that, *surface* beauty, there exists a beauty that can be generated by sanctity. So, too, can there be different kinds of eating. "Jewish eating" is different from ordinary eating. Jews are not lions! That is a truth to which the other details in the list will point.

AND BECAUSE YOU TOOK US OUT FROM THE LAND OF EGYPT. This does not refer to our emancipation from slavery. That comes next when we celebrate the fact that God *redeemed us from slavery.*

What is so bad about living in Egypt?

Here is what I believe.* I think that this part of the *berachah* is based on Devarim 11:10–12 as the Ramban (there) interprets it. The passage is pointing out the difference between living in Egypt and living in Eretz Yisrael. Here is what it says: In Egypt, blessed as it is with the Nile that every year with absolute predictability overflows its banks, it is possible to live without prayer for rain. Irrigation is simply not problematic. For practical purposes, it is possible to forget completely about the Ribono shel Olam: *Who is God that I should listen to His voice?*

That is not the case in Eretz Yisrael. There, if one does not wish to starve, one must resort to prayer. Rain, as they say in Israel, is absolutely essential. As Chazal teach us, the keys to rainfall are exclusively in the hands of the Ribono shel Olam. Consequently, Eretz Yisrael is, needs to be, cannot be conceived as being anything other than, *a land upon which the eyes of God are fixed from the first of the year to the last.*

---

* The suggestions that I am going to make for interpreting this and subsequent phrases in the second *berachah* are my own ideas. I have no reason to suppose that anybody else has ever understood this *berachah* as I have done. I offer these thoughts to those of you readers who are looking for some way to break out of our habitual, thoughtless mode of *bentching* and think that taking the phrases as I am suggesting might be of help. Even if I have not hit upon the exact truth, I do not think that you would be risking much by joining me. I cannot imagine that any of the ideas that I am suggesting are actually wrong.

Thank God (ideally in Eretz Yisrael) for having taken us out of Egypt.

The constant awareness of the Ribono shel Olam engendered by the need for rain, and the fact that it is that rain which provides us with the food that we eat, makes the mention of the Exodus a natural inclusion in *Birkas HaMazon*.

YOU REDEEMED US FROM THE HOUSE OF BONDAGE. In part III of this book (see chapters 7–10), we deal at length with the implications of the *cheirus* (freedom, liberation) that we celebrate during *zeman cheiruseinu* (the time of our freedom, a synonym for Pesach). Still, it seems to me that in spite of the really careful analysis to which we subjected this concept, none of what we said there would explain why this ought to be part of our *Birkas HaMazon*. On the surface it does not seem to impact upon our eating, as does *yetzi'as Mitzrayim* (the Exodus), as we have just learned.

I believe that the solution lies in Tehilim 81, the psalm that we recite every Thursday. There we read in verse 7, which speaks of what happened as a result of our emancipation, *I freed his shoulders from carrying burdens; his hands would no longer reach for the pot.* It is difficult to accommodate the reference to the pot. What exactly is meant? Some of the Rishonim (early authorities) suggest that when the Israelites ceased to be slaves they no longer had to cook for their masters. That is, of course, true. But why make an issue of it? I do not recall coming across any reference to an assumption that the onerousness of the Israelite slavery in Egypt was expressed in the kitchen. Why pick out cooking from any of the other chores that presumably they were called upon to carry out?

R. Samson Raphael Hirsch offers a different insight. He sees the centrality of eating, the obsessive interest in food, as a function of the mind-set of the slave. Bereft of any other freedom, he can at least dream of the next meal. God had hoped that by removing the dreadful burdens that crushed his body, by finally permitting him to stand up straight (*komemius*, see chapter 10), He would enable the erstwhile slave to shuck off such depressing single-mindedness. He would reach a stage of psychological well-being that would allow him to stop his hands from constantly "reaching for the pot."

That understood, our emancipation from slavery suddenly becomes very germane to our *Birkas HaMazon*. Food is indeed important in our lives, but it is not in any way "the" or even "a" supreme value.

I find it difficult to translate this phrase. I suppose that we ought to take the root word ם ת ח (*ch-t-m*) as, *to seal*. So what does it mean? That God *sealed a covenant in our flesh*? In what sense does circumcision "seal a covenant"?

Here is how I see it. The *berachah* that we recite at a *bris milah* reads "...*Who sanctified the beloved one from the womb, and placed the mark of the decree in his flesh, and* SEALED HIS OFFSPRING [THE DESCENDANTS OF HIS BELOVED] WITH THE SIGN OF THE HOLY COVENANT." For our purpose, the important phrase is the last one. The subject is God; the predicate is *He sealed*; the object is, *the descendants of His beloved*.* So it is people that are being sealed. Now that formulation makes a lot of sense. "Sealing" is to be taken as *bringing to a conclusion*. The sense is that Jewish males are born incomplete. Uncircumcised, they are missing something in their very essence. The removing of the foreskin creates perfection.

Since we have established from the phrase *sealed his offspring [the descendants of His beloved] with the sign of the holy covenant*, that the sealing is accomplished by a sign of the holy covenant, we are forced to take the word *bris* in the phrase *for Your covenant (bris) that You sealed in our flesh* as a shortened form of *os bris kodesh, the* SYMBOL OF THE COVENANT *that confers sanctity*. That accomplished, we can make the same assumption in our *Birkas HaMazon*. The phrase, *for Your covenant (bris) that You sealed in our flesh* is to be understood as though it had been written, *for the* SYMBOL OF THE COVENANT. We are thanking God for having provided us with a sign that our bodies have been brought to perfection.

---

* Either Yitzchak or Avraham see Rashi and Tosafos to Shabbos 137b.

The curbing of the fiercest expression of physical desires that is implicit in the act of circumcision is of course com-

pletely at home in the second *berachah* as we have explained it. If we can control that to some extent, we can make sure that our eating will be more civilized. Or, let us state clearly what we really mean. It will enter a level at which we can dream of touching holiness.

AND FOR YOUR TORAH WHICH YOU TAUGHT US... Does the Torah take a stand about what our attitude to eating should be? Is it something to be enjoyed? Ought we to delight in the delicious flavors that are available to us either naturally or through the arts of a talented cook, or ought we to bring ourselves to the table pretty much as we bring our cars to the gas station? That is a very important question.[1]

I suppose that we could cite a number of *berachos* that seem very clear on this subject. First among them would be the one that we recite in the spring when the first blossoms appear on the trees: *That nothing is lacking in His world, and He created it with good creations and good trees in which human beings can delight.* And there are many more.[2] Still, on that basis alone, it seems to me that we ought not to jump to any conclusions. Even the *delight* that is mentioned in this *berachah* does not refer to gobbling down the tasty fruit but to delighting in the profligacy and beauty of nature's openhanded generosity. There are other experiences involved in being refreshed by a crunchy apple besides the lip-smacking taste.

Let us listen to the rebbi of our generation, the great and holy Chazon Ish, as he advises a *ben Torah* how best to discharge his duties in this world.* Here is an excerpt from section 1 that stands at the very head of the list.

Try hard not to eat for pleasure...such indulgence is more harmful to the soul than is any halachic uncleanliness for the body...[the propensity to indulge in food

* *Igros Chazon Ish*, 1:20.

comes] from a lowly place [and it] hinders the ability to learn, as it says in the Midrash, Rather than pray that Torah should enter your mind, pray that luxuries not enter your body. The Gemara teaches that it were best to avoid any meal that seems particularly delicious to you.*

Now, we are all aware of the fact that private letters such as this one are to be handled with care. We do not know the young man to whom this letter was addressed and must consider the possibility that this particular piece of advice has no general validity but was fitted to the needs of that particular person. Still, my intuition tells me that this passage is so obviously packed with conviction that we are safe in assuming that it represents the Chazon Ish's actual conviction. Please take the time to glance at endnote 1. Quite a lot seems to be demanded of us if we take our *Yiddishkeit* seriously.

Still, there are also other perspectives from which the convergence of Torah and physical indulgence can be viewed. In Maharal's thought, great significance attaches to Pesachim 68b, which teaches that although one who feels that his spirituality would be enhanced by fasting would be permitted to refrain from eating on Pesach and Sukkos, that is not true of Shavuos: *All agree that eating is mandatory on Shavuos. It is the day upon which we received the Torah.* Here is a quote from Tiferes Yisrael 25 that provides background to this idea.

Kidushin 30b teaches that the Torah can be compared to a life-giving elixir. It can be thought of in the following terms. A man once beat his son and inflicted a grievous wound upon him. He covered the wound with some medication and said, "My son, as long as you keep this on your wound, you can eat whatever you want. You can bathe in either hot or cold water. However, if you re-

---

* This quote is taken from *Gittin* 70a. I am not quite sure why the Chazon Ish considered it germane to his thesis. A careful reading of that *sugia* seems to place this piece of advice in the area of healthy living. If you enjoy a certain food very much you will tend to overeat and harm your health. The ethical thrust with which the Chazon Ish imbues it seems not to be yielded by the context.

move it, the wound will fester." Thus, too, did God speak: "My children, I created an evil inclination which can endanger you, but also provided you with the Torah that can serve as an antidote. As long as you immerse yourself in Torah study you have nothing to fear from this evil inclination...but if you choose not to immerse yourself in Torah study, you will be helpless to withstand its cajoling.

The Torah protects us from our evil inclination. It is for this reason that on Shavuos, the day we received the Torah, the service in the Beis HaMikdash involved *chametz* (symbolic of physical enjoyment). On Shavuos...because the evil inclination is powerless, we have nothing to fear....When Torah is present there is no need to keep physicality distant.

So Torah provides a safety zone within which we can enjoy the bounties that the Ribono shel Olam built into His beautiful world. As we learned earlier, this Torah guarantees that we will not sink into an animal-like self-indulgence.

Torah has earned its place in the second *berachah*.

FOR LIFE, GRACE, AND LOVING-KINDNESS THAT YOU GRANTED US. The context in which this phrase appears—the second *berachah*—makes it clear that the "us" of the phrase "You granted us" refers to *klal Yisrael*. So God freely granted [חנן] us, the Jewish people, life. But clearly we are not the only people who are alive. So in what way is our life special? Because of this I am persuaded that the combination, חיים חן וחסד is to be translated, *a life imbued with grace and loving-kindness.**

What do these two terms mean? We could go to Megilas Esther to find out. Upon her arrival in Shushan, Esther immediately made a favorable impression (*Vatisa chesed lefanav*)

---

* The fact that the word *chein* lacks a conjunctive *vav* tends to bear this out. If these qualities were to be taken as three separate gifts, we would have expected to see *v'chen*, the "v" meaning "and."

upon Heigai,* the official in whose charge she was placed (Esther 2:9). In fact, everybody seems to have been attracted to her ("And Esther found *chein*, grace, in the eyes of all who saw her"—Esther 2:15). So they describe a winsome amiable, personality, someone who is universally loved and admired.**

We seem to be really nice people.

How does that come about?

In the sources available to me, I did not find any commentators who addressed our phrase, except for *Iyun Tefillah* (printed in the *Otzer HaTefillos*). He notes that Devarim 4:1 and 8:1, both promise that "life" is granted to us as a result of having been given the Torah.*** Now, as we noted above, that seems to be problematic. There are, after all, a lot of people who are alive but are not Jewish. But, let us remember that the phrase that we are discussing follows hard upon the earlier one that thanks God for the Torah He has taught us and the usages with which He has acquainted us, and with that we have our answer. It is impossible to live a life nurtured by the Torah's standards without being imbued with the kindness and consideration towards God and man that are the driving force, more or less directly, that underlie all the *mitzvos* and qualities that the Torah seeks to foster. We conclude that our phrase is a direct continuation of the earlier one: *for Your Torah that You have taught us that helped us attain a life filled with grace and loving-kindness.*

---

* We make bridegrooms happy by describing their brides as *na'eh vechasudah*. Rashi (Bereishis 39:21) makes clear that this does not mean that she is both beautiful and pious (that would have been expressed by using the term *chasidah*) but that she was everybody's friend.

** Obviously, this is only true of people who do not fall under the dreadful category of "It is a known fact that Esav hates Yaakov." (See *Rashi*, Bereishis 33:4)

*** At Devarim 4:1 we have, *Now, O Israel, listen to the decrees and to the ordinances that I teach you to perform, so that you may live.* At 8:1 we have, *All the commandment that I command you today you shall observe to perform, so that you may live.*

THE THIRD BERACHAH

I am not sure that any of the following is, strictly speaking, correct. It does not really matter too much, because all that I am looking for is a metaphor for what I am really trying to understand. So let us all just agree that, at least for our purposes, the following is true. Somewhere, let us say in Greenwich, England, there is a zealously guarded clock that is as accurate as human ingenuity can make it. All time-related issues concerning different zones and the like are based on that universally accepted standard. It has to be carefully guarded because within its own world it is "Truth" with a capital "T." And with truth you do not fool around.

We are ready to forget about metaphors and start talking practicalities. Here is a quote from the Maharal in *Gevuros HaShem* 47:

> God guards Yerushalayim constantly. He does not permit Himself even a moment's respite. He knows well that if He were to stop being concerned with its well-being, nobody could ever take His place. We have experienced that throughout our history. When the inhabitants of Yerushalayim act as the Ribono shel Olam would have us act, the city remains safe.

Please note! It is Yerushalayim, not the whole of Eretz Yisrael, that is the zealously guarded "atomic clock" in the explanation of the metaphor. Why?

Let me explain my question. The fact that there is a hierarchy of sanctity wherein Yerushalayim is holier than the rest of the land is of course readily granted. But that does not really answer the question that I raised. If sanctity were the criterion of what is to be specially protected, it is not readily clear why the cutoff point is Yerushalayim. Why not the *Har HaBayis* (the place where the Beis HaMikdash stood)? Why not the holiest of all? Why not the *Kodesh HaKodoshim* (the innermost sanctum of the Beis HaMikdash, where the ark rested)?

So apparently the unit that is of special interest to the Ribono shel Olam is the whole of Yerushalayim, including all the various levels of sanctity that it contains. If the metaphor that I have used is correct,* that would imply that "multilayered Yerushalayim" is the repository of a significant "Truth" that the Ribono shel Olam wants very much to keep safe. What Truth might that be?

I believe that the entire Yerushalayim complex, with all its various gradations in the measure of sanctity that defines them, is meant to encompass within itself all reality as it is able to be grasped by us. I believe that the *Kodesh HaKodoshim* represents the higher world, so to speak: God's world.[3] The city of Yerushalayim represents the created world within which we were placed and in which we function. The area reaching from the beginning of the Temple mount and extending through the entire area up to the *paroches* (embroidered curtains) that cordoned off the Holy of Holies represents the world of divine service, the conduit through which we humans reach up toward the unknowable, and through which the Ribono shel Olam, so to speak, reaches down to imbue our physical world, to the extent to which this is possible, with an aura of Godliness.

So what does all that have to do with *Birkas HaMazon*?

For that we have to go to Bava Basra 25b: Said Rabbi Yitzchak, One who wants to grow wise should turn to the south. [One who wants] to grow rich should turn to the north, represented by the fact that the *shulchan* (upon which sat the showbread) was located in the North and the menorah in the south. The menorah that stood in the southern part of the Heichal was the source from which all wisdom flowed. If it is wisdom that we crave, we would do well to concentrate upon the southern Heichal. The table with its showbread arranged upon it, which stood in the northern section, played a similar

---

* This is something that I cannot guarantee. It seems legitimate enough for me, but I have not seen it in any *sefer* nor heard it in any *shiur*. Please be aware of this as you read on.

role for our physical possessions. God's providence flows to us through the agency of that part of the Beis HaMikdash.

As is so often the case, a metaphor will turn out to be the most efficient way to make things clear. Let us imagine that American foreign policy makes it expedient to send aid to a given country. The most immediate needs are in education and nutrition. Congress assigns the amounts that will be devoted to each of these causes and the State Department, through the appropriate agency, will make those sums available. They will not send the money directly to schools and grocery stores. That is the job of the American embassy that is in place for this and similar needs. The embassy will have an Education section and a Nutrition section. These will have the knowledge and the wherewithal to distribute the largesse most efficiently and to the best advantage.

At this point, things should be clear. In the *nimshal* the *Kodesh HaKodoshim*—extra-territorial as we have explained earlier—is the Ribono shel Olam's embassy. The various departments through which the embassy functions are located in the Heichal. The menorah deals with Education; the *shulchan* carries responsibility for nutrition. Yerushalayim, the encampment of Israel, is where life actually takes place.

The third *berachah*, the one that deals with Yerushalayim and the Beis HaMikdash, is precisely where we would have expected it to be. Earlier in this chapter we established that the structure of *Birkas HaMazon* is based on a progression. We start in the first *berachah* as one of the crowd; we progress to the second one in which we examine the nature of "Jewish" eating. In the third *berachah* we round off those insights by tracing the ultimate source of our food to the Ribono shel Olam's "embassy" in the *Kodesh HaKodoshim*.

THE FOURTH BERACHAH

Does the fourth *berachah* fit into the scheme that we have plotted for *Birkas HaMazon*? It does have a different provenance than do the first three *berachos*,[4] but that of course does not mean that it was just stuck on without any regard for the integrity of *Birkas HaMazon* as a single and therefore necessarily coherent unit.

If you have consulted endnote 4, as I hope you have, you will have learned that the fourth *berachah* was ordained in Yavneh in recognition of God's goodness, which was evidenced when those who were killed in Beitar during Bar Kochba's abortive rebellion against the Romans were brought to burial. For years that was impossible because of the enemy's relentless siege. Miraculously, throughout those terrible years, none of the bodies decomposed. They were ultimately buried with the dignity and respect they deserved.

Certainly we can understand why a *berachah, hatov vehameitiv,* was in place. But why in *Birkas HaMazon?* What does death, miraculous preservation, and ultimate burial have to do with my lunch?

I hope that I can get you to agree with me on what I am about to suggest. After all the groundwork that we have laid, it seems to me that the answer is obvious. Why, after all, are we so careful to show respect to the dead body? Nothing of the soul is left; what lies before us can really be regarded as not much more than the sum total of the food that has been consumed throughout a lifetime. And that truth is exactly that for which we are searching. Like the fourth movement in a symphony, the fourth *berachah* is the crescendo toward which the first three *berachos* have struggled.

The fourth *berachah* leaves us no doubt. Our eating is a holy eating. Our bodies, even after death, are holy bodies. We are—never doubt it—a holy people!

Birkas HaMazon can be a life-altering experience. Let us try hard not to waste it.

6.

The Fourth Berachah

*T*heory is one thing; practice is another. We *did* get somewhere in the previous chapter, did we not? Having a solid sense of the entire, really very complex, Birkas HaMazon is no small matter. But, until we discipline ourselves to actually get involved in what we are saying, it is not a particularly large matter either. What are we going to do in order to grow up?

Here is an idea for those of you who would like to improve your *bentching* performance and experience. Why not set aside Shabbos as the day that will host your efforts at gradual improvement? It makes sense on a superficial level but, as I was mulling it over, it struck me that even beneath the surface, a marriage between *Birkas HaMazon* and Shabbos seems to be very much a *shidduch* made in heaven.

In the first place, Shabbos is a day on which we have time. Under normal circumstances we are not rushing anywhere and, if we are because we cannot wait to get to bed, our Shabbos anyway needs a lot of fixing.[1] So from that standpoint alone it would make sense to set aside the three times we *bentch* on Shabbos for some responsible and serious communication with the Ribono shel Olam.

But there is more, much more. It seems to me that Shabbos and *Birkas HaMazon* are pretty much identical twins. Both are charged with discovering and then revealing the essential, deeply significant reality that nestles within an outer form that appears to belie that truth. We have covered that aspect of *Birkas HaMazon* in the previous chapter and there is no need to go over it once more. What we need to do briefly now is to show that Shabbos has that same function.

Why only briefly? Because a detailed exploration could

fill many books and, even if I had the ability, which I do not, that would not be practical in the present context. I will just share with you a number of insights that I learned from Rav Hutner's *Pachad Yitzchak* on Shabbos.

Rav Hutner returns again and again to the Ga'on's assertion that God's rest is absolute and complete. On Shabbos He does nothing at all that is in any way creative. We have a tradition that God re-creates the world every single day.* On Shabbos even that creative act ceases.

That, of course, is an assertion that shocks. We all know perfectly well that nature does not miss a beat on Shabbos. How can the world function in every way that it does on other days if the Ribono shel Olam "rests" from His daily creative function of re-creation?

Rav Hutner offers a brilliant solution. He takes the forbidden act of carrying out in the street as a paradigm. Now to have transgressed the Torah sanction against carrying, let us say food, a reasonable amount (as determined by *halachah*) must be involved. Less than that amount would not count.* Now let us picture the following eventuality. Our friend, Reuven, for some reason requires a small amount of food (too small to really matter) across the road. He puts it on a plate and carries it over. Now, the food is out of the picture because there is just not enough of it. What about the plate? Is he liable for that?

The halachic answer is that, if he does not need the plate over there for any other purpose than providing a "handle" for the food, he is not liable.

To sum up: In order to qualify as a *melachah*, under the rules of creative, intended work, the action must be undertaken for its own sake. If that is not the case, if the plate is not needed but only the food that is on it, carrying the plate would not qualify as a *melachah*.**

For Rav Hutner, the problem with the Ga'on's assertion that

---

* By rabbinic decree even less would be interdicted, but, let us keep things as simple as we can.

** המוציא אוכלין פחות מכשיעור בכלי פטור אף על הכלי שהכלי טפלה לו (Shabbos 93b).

God "rested" on Shabbos from all involvement in the running of our physical world is solved. During the week, the physicality of our physical world holds center stage. Involvement in running it would qualify as a *melachah* in the fullest sense of the word. On Shabbos, the world's soul, not its body, predominates. It is true that even on Shabbos nature goes its normal way, and it is equally true that it can do so only because the Ribono shel Olam is *re-creating it each day*. But that does not contradict the fact that the Ribono shel Olam "rests" on Shabbos. The physical becomes totally subordinate to the soul of the day. Whatever is done at that level cannot—and, plate-like, does not—rise to the status of creative work.

Very clearly, Shabbos and *Birkas HaMazon* are on the same page. Both insist that there exist entire universes of truths beneath the truth. For *Birkas HaMazon* we spent the entire previous chapter trying to show that this is the message that *Birkas HaMazon* sends our way. For Shabbos, we have just apprehended its centrality. At root, they both deflect our attention from the physical (which in itself is, of course, perfectly legitimate) to a spiritual level, which, in the end, is a truer truth.

The late great R. Yisrael Salanter* used to bemoan the fact that "We tend to swallow the Shabbos together with the *tzimmes*." I suppose that today we might say, "If you don't watch out you can drown Shabbos in the *cholent* pot." It all comes to the same thing. The good food that we eat on Shabbos is there to awaken us to the exalted character of this holy day, not to deflect our attention from it.

With only a minimum of thought and energy, we should be able to pummel our *bentching* and our Shabbos into a fruitful and symbiotic relationship. Please do not take this personally (or rather, do take it personally!), but most of us need a *chizuk* in our Shabbos observance (please make a point of rereading endnote 1 in this chapter). Ditto for our *bentching*. Here is how they could interact. Certainly mulling over all the insights that *bentching* offers us that we discovered in the

---

* Quoted by R. Dessler in *Michtav MeiEliyahu*, volume 1, page 227.

previous chapter could have a salutary effect on the way we experience Shabbos. And Shabbos will be delighted to reciprocate. As your Shabbos becomes more meaningful, your delight in meeting up with aspects of your Jewishness that you have never experienced before will surely help you to anticipate *bentching* time with a happy excitement that will replace whatever it is that is happening now.

PART III

Pesach

7.

Tasting Matzah

*W*e all know pretty much what Pesach is all about, so there does not seem to be a pressing urgency to submit the issue to the very careful analysis that we have tried to set as the standard for the chapters in this book. All right, there are obviously depths and profundities beneath the surface,* but, few of us should be having dealings with *sisrei Torah*, the *esoteric truths* that lurk somewhere other than in the open text. I suspect that most of us are *"peshat Yidden"* and, with *peshat* most of us are reasonably familiar.

Except that, at least as far as I am concerned, I have just found out that this is simply not true. As I began to think through some of my assumptions, I discovered to my horror that even many of the most elementary components of this wonderful Yom Tov were a total mystery to me. So, once more, we are back to the problem we have faced again and again throughout this book. We seem to understand least those matters that we thought we knew best. Our curiosity has been dulled by years of rote performance. Of course we all like to hear a *"gut vort,"* a sparkling insight, but to the profundities that nestle in the well-worn and familiar, our minds are often closed.

Let us grow up and try to experience the Ribono shel Olam's Torah as it should be experienced. Let all parts of it be always new in our eyes.

---

* As there are in every word, indeed, in every letter of the Torah.

MATZAH

So let us begin with something really simple. At least we all know what matzah is, don't we? This we can take for granted and we can carry on from there. Except that, once more, we can't.

Let us begin at the beginning.

From the Torah and from the siddur we are familiar with the term *Chag HaMatzos*. I never before questioned this, but now I do. Here is why. If I would ever have been challenged to define "matzah," I would have done so in purely negative terms. It is bread that never had a chance to rise: as they say in English, "unleavened bread." What is so great about unleavened bread that the entire Yom Tov should be named in its honor? After all, Rambam (*Chametz U'Matzah* 6:1) makes very clear that after the first night when, as we learn in the Haggadah, we eat it in memory of the speed with which we had to leave Egypt,* eating matzah is a matter of pure choice.** There seems to be absolutely no reason why, after the first night, we should touch a piece of matzah until next year's Seder.

Matzah's claim to fame always seemed to me to be true in only negative terms. *Chametz* is forbidden and matzah is not *chametz*, and so it can be eaten on Pesach, but that is all. In what way can the rest of Yom Tov, after the first night, be considered to be a *Chag HaMatzos*? If we are going to define the Yom Tov in terms of what may or may not be eaten, it will turn out to be much more a time of *not* eating *chametz* than it is *for* eating matzah.

* Since the dough of our forefathers did not have sufficient time to rise.
** Mishnah Berurah points out that matzah after the first night is more a matter of choice than is succah after the first night. It is true that once that first meal has been eaten, there is no more obligation to eat in the succah unless we choose to eat a meal that has the status of *keva*, a proper meal, but then on Yom Tov we are required to eat a proper meal, and therefore to some extent the succah obligation extends beyond the first night. That is not the case with matzah because, although on Yom Tov we are obliged to eat bread, that could be done with matzah *ashirah*, a form of matzah that does not qualify for the matzah of mitzvah.

Now, many of us are aware of the fact that there is a tradition that the Vilna Ga'on held that although there is no *obligation* to eat matzah during the rest of Yom Tov, one who does do so fulfills a mitzvah.[1]* It seems to me that this same idea is expressed by Chizkuni to Shemos 12:18.

> There are actions for which you receive reward when you perform them and punishment when you don't. For example, eating matzah on the first night of Pesach. There are other actions for which you are rewarded when you do them, but there is no punishment when you do not, for example, eating matzah the rest of Pesach. However, regarding the mitzvah of matzah, it says, "Seven days shall you eat matzah." Hence, if you eat matzah during all these seven days, you act in accordance with the verse that states, "Seven days shall you eat matzah."**

If that is so, then of course our problem is solved. My assumption about the negative definition of matzah is shown to be flawed. Matzah has value in its own right.

This is powerful stuff. Pesach appears to be taking on a shape and significance that many of us have never before suspected. Let us work out the implications. We will begin by reminding ourselves why we are commanded to eat matzah on Seder night. Here is what the Haggadah says:

> Why do we eat matzah? Because our fathers' dough did not have time to rise before the King of Kings, the Holy One blessed be He, revealed Himself and redeemed us. As it is written, "They baked the dough that they brought out of Egypt, loaves of matzah, because it never

---

* Here is the language of the *Mishnah Berurah* 475:45: The Vilna Ga'on is of the opinion that it is a mitzvah to eat matzah every day of Pesach, but it is not an obligation.

** In many printed versions of Chizkuni, the text of this passage is corrupt and makes no sense at all. I have used the text, based on a reliable handwritten manuscript, used by Rav Chavel in the Mosad HaRav Kook edition of the Chizkuni.

became leavened. [This was because] the Jews had been driven out of Egypt and they could not delay. They did not even have time to prepare food for the journey.

Now this appears to be an unequivocal statement. This reason, and none other, is why we eat matzah. We certainly are not going to suggest that on the first night we eat matzah for the reason given, but that the voluntary "mitzvah" of the rest of the Yom Tov has some other rationale. We are not given any license to dream up ideas of our own. So why would it be meritorious to eat matzah the rest of Pesach because we *had* to eat in on the first?

WHY DO WE REALLY EAT MATZAH?

So it is quite clear that it is meritorious to eat matzah every day of Pesach, because we *had* to eat it on the evening of the first. So here is a question: Which way do the arrows point? Is it: You were in a rush *therefore* → eat matzah! Or is it: I made sure that you would leave Egypt in a rush ← *because it was important to Me that* you eat matzah? Did the dough not rise because we were in a rush, or were we in a rush in order that the dough should not rise? Upon reflection, I think that we would incline toward the latter of the two alternatives. It goes against the grain to suggest that the Ribono shel Olam could not have slowed things down a bit in order that the people could take along some really delicious sandwiches for the trip.

So, for the moment, we have decided that we were rushed in order that the dough should not rise. Now what does *that* mean? What is so great about the dough not rising?

We are approaching some very holy ground. Let us tread carefully. We are going to be learning two Maharals from the *Gur Aryeh* and I have the feeling that, after that, our experience of Pesach will never again be the same.

Let us go to Shemos 12:17 where we have a very cryptic *pasuk*. Here is an approximate rendering: *Make very sure to guard against the matzos [becoming* chametz] *for it was on this very day that I brought out your hosts from Egypt.*

Here is Rashi:

And you shall guard the matzos that they should not rise. From here, [the sages] said that if it shows signs of rising, inhibit the process with cold water. Rav Yoshiya says, "Don't read the word as *matzos*, but rather, as *mitzvos*. Just as we don't permit the matzos to become leavened, so we don't permit the *mitzvos* to become leavened. If you have the opportunity to perform a mitzvah, do it right away.

Both parts of this Rashi require attention. Both are carefully considered by Maharal, as we shall see. In the meantime, here is something to think about. What is the connection between the two parts of the *pasuk*? Why does the fact that the Ribono shel Olam took us out of Egypt on *that very day* make it essential that our matzos do not become *chametz*? Keep this question in mind; we will try to have an answer before we bring this chapter to a close.

Here is the first of the two Maharals that we will be learning.

Prevent any leavening. This means that one should not say, "As I am only commanded not to have *chametz* [I don't have to be too careful]. [After all, if the dough threatens to become *chametz*,] I can always burn it right away." Therefore it says, *And you shall guard the matzos*— Do not rely on burning it later. You must be vigilant that it should not become *chametz* in the first place.

If you have looked at this Maharal carefully, you will have picked up that he is discussing the very issue that we raised a few lines ago. Is matzah simply bread that was not allowed to rise and therefore is not *chametz*, but, as matzah, has no statement to make? Or is it something that has independent significance? Rashi, as Maharal reads him, provides the answer. If the first of the two alternatives were correct, if matzah as matzah had no intrinsic value other than that it can be eaten on Pesach, there would be no harm in permitting the dough to become *chametz*. It can be immediately burned and no harm would have been done. Only if matzah *as* matzah has meaning can we understand the Torah's prohibition against allowing it to become *chametz*.

Even without as yet understanding what the innate value of matzah might be, we can see that we are standing on the threshold of mighty revelations. We headed this section by asking why we really eat matzah. Can you imagine what it will do to our future celebrations of Pesach to find out, to *really* find out, what we are doing when we eat a piece of matzah?

Things are heating up. Let us continue.

I will now paraphrase the second Maharal:

The plain meaning of the verse is clearly that we are not to permit the dough that we are baking to become leavened. Still, by leaving out any explanation for *why* we are to "guard" the matzos, the Torah hints at a different meaning that can be read out of the text. "*Mitzvos*, too, are to be protected from any "leavening"!

What can that possibly mean? And why would Rashi bring a Chazal that seems to throw no light at all upon the simple meaning of the text?

Chazal are pointing out that there is an affinity between matzos and *mitzvos*. Delay is the enemy of both; speed is their friend. The passage of time is a function of the physical. God acts outside the "time" framework. We humans can get to some approximation of that timelessness only by doing things as quickly as we can. On Pesach where the Ribono shel Olam was Himself involved in the process of redemption, and because of the Ribono shel Olam's involvement the process was timeless, things have to move as quickly as they can.

Mitzvos share that characteristic. A delayed mitzvah is a defective mitzvah. If a command is really to be a "command," there is no time for dilly-dallying.*

---

* Please take the time to study the last section of the introduction carefully. There we discuss why a delayed mitzvah is a deficient mitzvah.

There is so much to say at this point that we have to pace ourselves carefully. Let us first spell out the answer to the question that we asked a couple of paragraphs back. We wondered what the connection might be between the two phrases at Shemos 12:17 that we have been discussing. Why do we have to carefully protect the dough that we are kneading *because* it was on this very day that the Ribono shel Olam took us out from Egypt? What is the connection?

Now, of course, we know the answer; it lies in the words *this very day*. We asked earlier, "What was the hurry?" The answer is: "The 'hurry' was the hurry!" The Ribono shel Olam "Himself" was on the scene and the passage of time that allows for the luxury of a slow, expansive development is alien to His world. Speed as the "vernacular" of the Divine is the controlling element of what makes Pesach what it is.[2] Please take the time to read endnote 2.

We wondered why the entire Yom Tov of Pesach should be called *Chag HaMatzos* when the significance of the matzah seems to have been conditioned by events that took place on only the first of the seven days.

Let us get back to those confusing arrows that we used earlier. We came to a conclusion of sorts, but now the time has come to revisit the matter and nail down some ideas more firmly than we have been able to do until now.

Meet the arrows!

→ The past determines the future: the Jewish people had to rush out of Egypt, *consequently* the dough did not rise.

← What needs to happen in the future determines what has to happen now. It was required that, later on, the dough should not rise. *To guarantee that this would happen,* the Ribono shel Olam rushed them out of Egypt before that issue arose.

↔ Or, perhaps the correct symbol would be the bidirectional arrow? Both points, each within the context of its own reality, have validity.

I vote for the third symbol. I believe that only this one can help us out of the following quandaries, ones that we already discussed earlier in this chapter. Somehow we are going to have to accommodate two apparent opposites:

1. Matzah, given the reason for eating it that the Torah ascribes, is solidly tied to the first day only.
2. The appellation, *Chag HaMatzos*, announces loud and clear that the entire seven days are permeated by the matzah idea.
   Those two facts appear to contradict each other.

That is one way of putting the problem. Here is another.

A. The Torah's mitzvah to eat matzah is limited to the first night.
B. No, it is not. Not really. A number of verses indicate clearly that the Ribono shel Olam values our eating matzah the entire Yom Tov. So the mitzvah seems to apply throughout the seven days. But the fact is that it does not. Only one solution is possible. We do not have to eat matzah beyond the first night, but it is meritorious if we do.
   Those are the mechanics. Where is the soul?

We have learned that there are two ways of posing the problem. Where do we head for a solution that will fit either or both?

Enter our arrows. Or rather, enter the profound realities for which our silly little arrows stand as symbols. There is an outer form and an inner energy. Both arrows pointed in *a* correct direction. Neither tells the *whole* truth. There is no doubt that the *form* of what happened accorded with the Haggadah's description. The people were hounded out of Egypt so fast that there was no time to allow their bread to become leavened. We eat matzah on the first night of Pesach to commemorate that experience.

There is also no doubt that the spiritual energy of God's

will wrought its purpose in the opposite direction. As the Maharal that we quoted earlier makes clear, the events of that holy night were attuned to the Presence of the Ribono shel Olam, which, on that night, was more real and more awesome than at other times. That Presence demanded that the shackles of time be sundered. As near as is possible in our physical world, the passage of time had to be defied. The bread of Pesach needed to be matzah. Things would have to move with unusual speed if that necessary end was to be achieved. However, that aspect of the event was not *experienced* by the masses. No doubt there were those who knew and understood what was happening, but also no doubt many did not. Because of this, that energy is not immortalized in a formal mitzvah. It is enough that the Torah hints at what it hints. The Ribono shel Olam has revealed His preference. More is not required.

We have reached a point at which we have discovered a great deal more about matzah than we ever imagined we might require. We now know that it is not simply a non-*chametz* bread that can be used to make our meals more filling. It quite literally carries the spirit and instruction of Pesach on its back.

We are now in a position to give a more intelligent answer than we could have in the past to the following Pesach quiz: What are we to derive from our seven (or eight) Pesach days? How is the Pesach celebration and experience meant to impact upon our Jewishness? Is the value of Pesach self-contained or is it meant to send us onward and upward toward goals that we will still need to define?

We have come a long way. Let us leave these issues to some other chapters.

8.

THERE IS A STORY
BENEATH THE STORY OF
The Exodus from Egypt
LET US SEE IF WE CAN FIND IT

Stories are much like people. A cursory glance can yield a respectable, even partially true, perspective. But there is no doubt that many subtleties are tucked away in hidden places. To find those, there is no substitute for careful study.

Let us go treasure hunting in the *parshiyos* of *yetzi'as Mitzrayim* and see whether we can penetrate the surface. There really must be more to it than the story that we learned as children.

We begin with Shemos 12:23: *HaShem will pass through to smite Egypt, and He will see the blood that is on the lintel and the two doorposts; and HaShem will pass over the entrance and He will not permit the destroyer to enter your homes to smite.*

On *He will not permit* Rashi comments: *He will not permit him (i.e., withhold from him) the ability to come.* We are not to translate, *He will withhold permission,* but, *He will withhold the ability.* Maharal explains Rashi's thinking. The text need not stress the obvious. The story itself makes clear that the Destroyer (*mashchis*), whoever he might be, would not have *permission* to enter the Jewish homes. If anything needed saying, it must be that he did not even have the ability. The Jewish homes were simply closed to him.

Is there really a difference? Why would the withholding of permission not be sufficient? What are the implications? What are we being taught here?

I have the feeling that this question needs to be tackled in a broader context. We will set this question aside for the moment and take a little detour. We will return to the original question a little further along in this chapter.

The story of the plagues that were unleashed upon the Egyptians contains an element that, to the best of my knowledge, does not figure, at least not as prominently, in other contexts. I refer to the *miracles* within *the miracles* that were an apparently important feature of the Egyptian saga.

The plagues of blood and darkness provide examples.

For the plague of blood, we have Tanchuma, Vaeira which reports that if an Egyptian and a Jew were to simultaneously drink from the same cup, the Jew would drink water, while the Egyptian drank blood. In one form or another, this same thought is repeated in many different midrashim. A number of commentators* make a similar point in their comments to the plague of darkness. As they read the text, things went far beyond the fact that darkness did not descend upon the areas inhabited by Jews. They interpret the word *in their lodgings* in the phrase that *All* benei Yisrael *had light in their lodgings* to refer to the *Egyptian* homes. The very rooms that for the Egyptians were stuffed with masses of impenetrable darkness remained unaffected for the Jews in that same place. For them, the very same rooms that imprisoned the Egyptians in suffocating darkness remained as bright and welcoming as always.

Let us not be grabby. Let us live with the fact that we cannot have the slightest understanding of the ways in which these impossible-to-imagine situations were brought about. But, even if we are willing to give up on the "How?" we cannot oblige on the "Why?" The Ribono shel Olam is not a conjurer, intent upon wowing His audience with yet another rabbit drawn from some impossible hat. If it happened thus, we must conclude that the *yetzi'as Mitzrayim* that the Ribono shel Olam wanted could not have happened otherwise. Something vital to the entire enterprise would have been missing.

What is that?

What is the story beneath the story?

What was it that *yetzi'as Mitzrayim* needed to be that required that the physically impossible should somehow come about? What is Pesach all about? When we get right down

---

* See, for example, Rashbam and Chizkuni.

to it, was there not a more efficient way to determine who inhabited the house than *passing over* those that had been marked by the blood? What is so great about *passing over* and why should the entire Yom Tov owe its name to that particular aspect of an event that surely could have been viewed and honored in many different ways?

Earlier in this chapter I predicted that we would get to some of the answers to the problems that we had raised as we got further along in this chapter. I see now that that is not going to happen. We will have to be patient a little longer. We have some very important work ahead of us.

9

The Pesach Offering

*L*et us tackle first things first. What does Pesach mean? Rashi (Shemos 12:23), while quoting Targum (*to show mercy*), appears personally to favor, *to pass over*. So *pass over* it will be for us, and we have confirmed what we really knew all along. When we speak of "Pesach" we speak of the Ribono shel Olam "passing over" the Jewish homes, as He smote the Egyptians on that fateful night of our emancipation.

How important was this "passing over" in the broad picture of our redemption? The object of our celebration is, of course, the Exodus, *the emancipation from slavery*. On this vast and variegated canvas, what overarching significance could attach to the particular method by which the Ribono shel Olam made sure that the Jewish people should not be ravaged when all the firstborn were killed? It does not appear to be more than a detail. Moreover, we don't really understand so well why the whole procedure of the protective blood was necessary. When Egypt's dogs earned immortality by their silence as we were leaving, they did not need any identifying symbols to know whom to spare from their barking. Did the Ribono shel Olam Himself, did the heavenly *mashchis*, the angel charged with the actual killing, really require a sign?

But, of course, my thinking is totally incorrect in this matter. Not only am I wrong in looking upon the *passing over* as a dispensable detail; it, on the contrary, stands at the very center of Exodus to the extent that the entire enterprise of freeing us from slavery would have meant much, much less had this wondrous event not imbued it with the magic of its touch.

That sounds like a daring statement. Can I substantiate it?

Let us learn some verses together and stand astounded by

an insight that until this week had altogether escaped me. Here is Devarim 16:2–3.

> You shall slaughter the Pesach Offering to HaShem, your God from the flock...
> You shall not eat leavened bread *with it* (*alav*). For seven days you shall, *because of it* (*alav*), eat matzah, the bread of affliction, for you departed Egypt in haste, so that you may remember the day of your departure from Egypt all the days of your life.

I have italicized the translations of the word *alav* as it appears in each of the two phrases that constitute verse 3. It is upon the meaning of this word in the context within which each is used that I wish to focus. I imagine that our intuition would tell us that, appearing, as they do, so closely together in the same verse, they would be identical in meaning. Chizkuni teaches us* ** that this is not the case.

He demonstrates from a number of examples that *alav* can be used both as *with* and as *because of*. He insists that the first time it appears in our verse it is to be rendered as the former, the second time, the latter.

What forced Chizkuni to search for a different meaning in the second phrase? That is, of course, simple. The pronoun "it"*** in the first phrase obviously stands for the Pesach Offering. We are not to eat *chametz* together *with* it. Now the logic of syntax surely demands that the pronoun in the second usage within the same sentence must have the identical meaning as the first. But here we are discussing the seven-day Yom Tov during which we are to eat matzah. Now the Torah cannot possibly mean that we are to eat matzah together *with* the Pesach Offering all the seven days, since that offering

---

* It is inexplicable to me why Rashi does not address this issue. I mention this problem although I have no solution to offer, in order to encourage you readers to try your hands at finding an explanation.

** Please reread endnote 2 to chapter 7 at this point.

*** The Hebrew *alav* is a combination of *al*, that means *together with*, and *av*, which is the pronoun *it*.

could not be eaten beyond the first night. There is no escape from rendering the second *alav* differently from the first.

Chizkuni's elegant solution for the linguistic issue is pure joy. However, far beyond the technicalities, it carries profound consequences. The implications that arise from it as far as the meaning of our Yom Tov is concerned absolutely boggle the mind.

It turns out that when, throughout the seven days, we voluntarily eat matzah, our minds are to turn to, of all things, the Pesach Offering! But why should they? WE eat matzah on Pesach as a reminder of the speed with which we left Egypt; we eat the Pesach Offering because it recalls God's *passing* over our homes. Why should eating matzah (voluntarily at that!) remind us of the Pesach Offering?

Earlier in this chapter I mentioned that I had been wrong for all those years during which I had thought that the Pesach Offering, and the bloodying of the doorposts that it facilitated, were local in nature, no more than, somehow necessary, aspects of the tenth plague. It had become obvious to me that, in fact, they stood at the very center of the celebration of our freedom.

How so?

It is "promise-fulfilling time" and we have reached a point at which we must consider the questions that we left unanswered in chapter 8. It is a really short chapter, so why not take the time to scan it right now so that all of us will be on the same page at the same time? If you took my advice, you will now be mulling over the central problem that we posed there. Why did Rashi insist that the *mashchis* was not only denied *permission* to enter our homes, but that he was actually *unable* to do so. We did not examine the implications. We have to do that now. Then there was the problem of the name, *Chag HaMatzos*. Why should the entire Yom Tov take its name from the fact that we left Egypt in a hurry?

Herewith, I offer my suggestions.

At Shemos 6:6–7 the Torah lists the promises that God made to us as the Exodus was about to begin. The list culminates with the promise that, as a result of the process, God would adopt us formally as *His* people.

What are the implications?

They are spelled out in Ha'azinu (Devarim 32:7–11). You would do well to study the passage inside. Here I will just quote myself from my recent book on Ha'azinu.

> Verses 8–9: These verses set the tone for understanding the dynamics of our history. We were literally put into this world to fight the battles of the Ribono shel Olam for His ultimate vindication. The seventy nations are the same people who, while they were still one family, sought to do battle with the Ribono shel Olam by building the tower. Splitting them into seventy nations did not change their craving to rid their world of God. It simply defanged them by making communication between them impossible. The Ribono shel Olam's weapon against them would be a *chosen people* WHOSE NATIONAL ETHOS WILL BE DETERMINED BY BEING BASED ON SEVENTY PEOPLE INSTEAD OF SEVENTY COUNTRIES. The battle lines are drawn.
>
> Verses 10–14: These verses set the stage for what is to follow....The fact that this survey begins with a glance back at the wilderness where the Ribono shel Olam "found" us is, of course, absolutely appropriate. If, as we claim, the theme of Ha'azinu is to juxtapose the two seventies, "ours" reckoned in people with no dependence upon any real estate, "theirs" expressed in terms of their seventy countries, then the fact that God first "found" us in the desert is vital to the argument. Really, it says it all!

We are indeed very, very different. That difference can become clear to us if we trace it back to its beginnings: the contract that Yaakov and Eisav forged during their struggles in their mother's womb.

Here is a paraphrase from Sefer Eliyahu Zuta.*

We are taught that while they were still in the womb, Yaakov and Eisav made a contract. Yaakov had explained to Eisav that in Olam HaBa there would be none of the physical pleasures in which Eisav delighted. From his point of view it was not a very exciting place. Perhaps he (Eisav) would agree to a trade. He would get the whole Olam HaZeh with no strings attached; Yaakov would be an eternal stranger in that world. In return Eisav would leave Olam HaBa to Yaakov.

This division had practical results. Here is the continuation of the above midrash.

When, as Yaakov was returning to Eretz Yisrael from his exile in Charan, Eisav came out to meet him, Eisav was shocked, and put out, by what he saw. Yaakov was returning as a wealthy man, blessed with a beautiful family, wives and children and all the necessary appurtenances. Eisav felt cheated. Olam HaZeh was supposed to be his alone. Yaakov, he supposed, would have to be a mendicant with absolutely nothing of his own. How was it possible that Yaakov should be showered with such riches?

Yaakov answered that it was all an undeserved gift from God.

The stress is on "undeserved." Eisav was correct in claiming that we have no rights at all down here.

That is the kind of nation that we are. We do not belong in this world, have no place to call our own,** use what we need without rights but on sufferance.[1] Born, as we were, in the desert, we have spent the vast majority of our national lives in

---

* Or possibly, Pirkei d'R. Eliezer. See critical apparatus to Mosad HaRav Kook's Yalkut Shimoni.

** Even in Eretz Yisrael we cannot be owners in the full sense of the word. See VaYikra 25:23: ‏.והארץ לא תמכר לצמתת **כי לי הארץ** כי גרים ותושבים **אתם עמדי**

the *desert of exile* (Yechezkel 20:35). It is a long, long story. It is too long for this book, indeed too long to be contained in the vastest of vast libraries.

Here we can only ask one modest question. If we do not belong here, what are we doing here? We need to quote a small snippet from Rav Hutner's profound thoughts about Maharal's assertion that, *the intellect (haseichel) is a stranger in this world*. The following passage is a paraphrase of a few lines from *Ma'amar* 11 of the *Pachad Yitzchak* on Chanukah:

> The appropriate home for the intellect is really in Olam HaBa. It is out of place down here. That of course creates a problem. If it does not belong here, why is it here?
>
> Imagine a wise man in a strange place; far away from his yeshiva, his library, his students and from the entire *milieu* that he treasures and loves. So why is he here? There can only be one explanation. He has come to share his spiritual riches with people who otherwise would have absolutely no access to them.
>
> He gains nothing by being here; he gives everything by being here.

If you reread chapter 8 when I asked you to earlier in this chapter, you will recall that I bundled two seemingly disparate issues together. I wondered why the *mashchis* was denied not only *permission* to enter the Jewish homes but also the very *ability* to do so, and I also found it noteworthy that the *miracle* within *the miracle** played such a significant role in the drama of the plagues.

I think that on the basis of what we have learned in the current chapter, we have the answer. Influenced by the language that I found useful in posing the problems in the previous chapter, we have discovered the "story beneath the story." Our emancipation from Egyptian slavery has implications

---

* The fact that the liquid in the beaker was *both* blood and water at the same time, why the Egyptian homes were both dark and light depending on who was doing the looking,

way beyond the fact that a slave people was finally freed after two hundred years of unrelieved servitude. It speaks of freedom from the cloying shackles of physicality. An alien people, denizen of a higher, nobler, holier world, suddenly takes up center stage in human affairs. History will have to learn some new skills and play with them by new rules. Or, better still, not play with them at all. Neither *mashchis* nor plague can touch them. For them, the delegated *mashchis* simply does not exist. What is blood for the Egyptians simply *is* not blood for them. It is sparkling, refreshing water. Egyptian darkness *is* Jewish light.

At the moment in which the Ribono shel Olam "passed over" the Jewish homes, He marked us as His *portion*. That is a freedom beneath a freedom.[2]

And that is the story of our "Matzah Yom Tov." It is the "Story" beneath the "story" for which, in these past few chapters, we have been searching! In our discussion earlier in this chapter of the Chizkuni's rendering of the second *alav*, we remained with a question. What possible reason could there be for eating matzah (voluntarily) throughout Pesach in order to remind us of the Pesach Offering that has no halachic function whatsoever after the first night?

Here is the answer, loud and clear. The Pesach Offering with its attendant *passing over* defines our peoplehood more clearly than does any other event in our history.

In the following chapter we are going to offer a brief summary of what we have learned about Pesach.

10.

Chasal Siddur Pesach

AFTER THE SEDER

*W*e have traversed much ground in these last three chapters and discovered aspects of *yetzi'as Mitzrayim* that, at least for me, were entirely new. We peeked behind the well-known facts—water turning into blood, darkness engulfing the Egyptian homes, the Jews safe in their houses during that dreadful night when death sauntered down Egypt's streets—and found new worlds. Even modest matzah was revealed as harboring depths of meaning that had up till now escaped me. All in all, I felt a sense of satisfaction. Obstacles had been overcome, challenges had been met, the sun was shining and all seemed well.

Then I began to wonder. I came to realize that there was much that was going on in our Pesach experience to which I had never given any thought but, once I noticed some of the details, left me baffled.

Come join me in my travels. After more years than I care to contemplate, I still feel like a stranger entering upon a promised land.

It is the first night of Yom Tov. Let us go to shul.

Here is what we find. These are the opening words of the formulaic middle *berachah* that is common to all the Yamim Tovim.

You have chosen us from among all the nations, You loved us and wanted us and You elevated us above all tongues. You sanctified us with Your commandments and You, our King, brought us close to Your service and called us by Your great and Holy name.

All of which means:

We are very, very special. We are chosen. Our very being brings satisfaction to the Ribono shel Olam. God lifted us beyond the rest of humanity. He permitted us entry into the spheres of the sacred by means of the commands through which He bound us, thereby bringing us close so that our lives might find expression in His service. Moreover, He paid us the ultimate compliment. He was willing to tie His fate to ours. We would be identified by means of our relationship to Him and He would become known in His world through His association with us.

That is a portentous opening salvo. What limit can there possibly be to the demands to which such a statement serves as an appropriate introduction? We can almost hear the excitement: "Batten down the hatches! Here they come!"

And what are those demands?

You, HaShem our God, gave us appointed times during which we are to rejoice, festivals and seasons during which we are to be happy.

Well, those do not seem to be too onerous. The Ribono shel Olam wants us to be happy. Now that is not so bad, is it?*[1]

So how is Pesach to be enjoyed? What is there about *yetzi'as Mitzrayim* that is calculated to make us happy?

That's easy! *And You gave us...this festival of matzos, the time of our freedom.* Pesach ushers in the season of our freedom.

It is great to be free, is it not?

Careful now! Does that *zeman cheiruseinu*, time of our freedom, not strike a sour note? Is that what Pesach really is? Is it just a negative, an absence of the onus of slavery, a license to sleep late, a joy at being able to dispose of our time and energies as we are inclined to do? If that is all that there is, it does seem rather bland, does it not?

We are entering some very tricky territory.

---

* For Rosh Hashanah and Yom Kippur, these references to joyous celebration are omitted.

What exactly did *yetzi'as Mitzrayim* do for us?

Well, we say *kri'as Shema* twice a day, so we know the answer to that one. *I am the Lord your God, who took you out of Egypt to be your Lord.* That is clear enough. But, now comes a nagging question: Does *to be your Lord* equal "freedom"?

Then we have the first of the Ten Commandments: *I am HaShem your Lord, who took you out of Egypt...*Let us take a look at the Mechilta.

"You shall have no other God but Me." Why does it say this? Isn't it enough to say, "I am the Lord, your God"? We can compare this situation to a king who takes over a country. When his new servants beg him to make laws for them, he refuses, saying, "Only after you have accepted My sovereignty can you meaningfully accept my laws, too, for if I am not your king, how then will you do my bidding? So, too, God said to the Jewish people. "I am the Lord your God, you shall have no other God but me. Once you accepted me as your God in Egypt, you accepted my commands."

Of course there are many other *pesukim* in the Torah that deliver the same message. So why did whoever worked on the wording of *Atah Vechartanu* pick *zeman cheiruseinu?*[2]

I walked around with this problem for a while without making any noticeable progress. Then one day I was thinking over some passages in the Haggadah and it struck me that, in fact, there are sources, as rich and as clear as the ones that I cited above, that seemed to point in precisely the opposite direction.

Let us use the *pesukim* taken from Devarim 26:5–8 upon which we base our retelling of the story of *yetzi'as Mitzrayim* on Seder night.

Then you shall call out and say before HaShem, your God, "An Aramean tried to destroy my forefather. He descended to Egypt and sojourned there, few in number, and there he became a nation—great, strong, and numerous. The Egyptians mistreated us and afflicted us, and placed hard work upon us. Then we cried out to HaShem, the God of our forefathers, and HaShem heard our voice and saw our affliction, our travail, and our oppression. HaShem took us out of Egypt with a strong hand and with an outstretched arm, with great awesomeness and with signs and with wonders.

It is all very clear, very much to the point. We suffered, we prayed, we were heard, and we were miraculously saved. There is not a whiff of any indication that there was any purpose, any plan of somehow changing or strengthening our ties to the Ribono shel Olam as a result of this experience. Even the additional *pesukim* that were read when the Beis HaMikdash was still standing speak only of the joys of non-slavery, nothing at all of contractual or even morally appropriate obligations.

He brought us to this place, and He gave us this land, a land flowing with milk and honey. And now, behold! I have brought the first fruit of the ground that You have given me, O HaShem. And you shall lay it before HaShem, your God, and you shall prostrate yourself before HaShem your God. You shall be glad with all the goodness that HaShem your God has given you and your household—you and the Levite and the proselyte who is in your midst.

Once we think along these lines, more and more supportive passages come to mind.

Let us join Moshe Rabbeinu standing at the burning bush when he was first called to his destiny:

HaShem said, I have indeed seen the affliction of My people that is in Egypt and I have heard their outcry because of the task masters, for I have known of their sufferings. I shall descend to rescue them from the hand of Egypt and to bring them up from that land to a good and spacious land, to a land flowing with milk and honey, to the place of the Canaanites, the Hittites, the Amorite, the Perizzite, the Hivvite, and the Jebusite. And now, behold! The outcry of the children of Israel has come to Me, and I have also seen the oppression with which the Egyptians oppress them. And now, go and I shall dispatch you to Pharaoh and you shall take My people the children of Israel out of Egypt.

And simplest and starkest of all, we have the clear statement in the Haggadah: *We were slaves to Pharaoh in Egypt, and HaShem our God took us out with a mighty hand and an outstretched arm.*

Where do we go from here? Is there anywhere to turn?

As a matter of fact there is. I have the feeling that if we really concentrate on what we are about to learn, we will gain some very important insights into the most basic of Jewish questions: what and who we are supposed to be and where the potentials for our relationship with the Ribono shel Olam might be able to lead us.

We are going to be taking a careful look at *parshas* BeChukosai. We will argue that its contents are determined by the fact that it is the closing chapter of *sefer* VaYikra/Toras Kohanim.[3]

We all know that, in general terms, we can divide BeChukosai into two sections. The first (*If you follow My commands...*) describes the best-case situation in which we, as a community, act as the Ribono shel Olam would have us act, such that our lives on our land will unfold in holy and blessed serenity. The second (*And if you do not listen to me...*) tells—without pulling any punches—the horrors that we can expect if we decide to go our own way.

We are going to focus on the first section.

I think it best to begin by quoting the Ramban on this passage (VaYikra 26:11–12). He will point us in the direction that we ought to follow. I am quoting only the last two paragraphs from an extremely long piece. In the earlier parts he explains in detail the absolute perfection of the life that the promises in this section predict. When he has done that, he continues as follows:

These blessings only come to be when all of Israel does the will of God. Then heaven and earth attain perfection. And there is no other place that the Torah enumerates such complete blessings; these are the terms of the compact between us and God. Neither individuals nor groups in Israel have ever had sufficient merit to attain such a complete state of blessing, therefore, our sages say these verses refer to the future; that the time of perfection and completion.

If indeed the description given here has no match in the Torah, if this is the very acme of what living in accordance with the Torah's expectations will deliver, we really ought to know why it appears just in this particular context. Why here and nowhere else?

Please take the time to read endnote 3 if you have not yet done so, or review it if you are already familiar with it. There you have the answer. It is this. Beginning at Yisro and running all the way between there and the end of VaYikra, the Torah has been describing what a priestly and holy nation will look like. The passage at the beginning of BeChukosai that we are thinking about brings the story of *yetzi'as Mitzrayim* to a close.

"This," the Ribono shel Olam is telling us, "is what I had in mind for you when I judged the time ripe to permit you to savor freedom. It is true that, on the basis of the contract that Yaakov made with Eisav while still in Rivkah's womb, you are no more than guests in this, My physical world. But you need not be ordinary guests. I can teach you to become visiting royalty. If you remember always that noblesse oblige,* if you remain determined to live by the standards of the palace

---

* *Noblesse oblige* is a French term that has found a welcome in the English language. It means that a claim to particular nobility carries obligations with it. (In modern Hebrew they borrowed the idea from the French but translated it *ha'atzilut mechyevet*, nobility comes wrapped in obligations.) Morally we have no choice but to act in ways that are appropriate to our high standing in society.

that is your real home, if you never allow your dreams to become tarnished, or your actions to make you ashamed, if you never forget who and what you really are, there will be no limits to the amenities that your temporary guest-house will offer you."

The first part of BeChukosai brings *yetzi'as Mitzrayim* to an end. After this final chapter in that world-shattering drama, we are ready to begin our history as a newly minted nation. We are ready to begin *sefer* BeMidbar—and to come face-to-face with the final paragraph in the Ramban that we quoted above. It is a sad account of dashed hopes and apparently ever-present and plaguing inadequacies. But that is another story for another time.

*   *   *

If you have read the first part of this chapter carefully, I would imagine that, to a degree, a feeling of anticipation has built up in you. We have, as it were, cleared the decks for action; we have identified the passage in the Torah where the secrets of *yetzi'as Mitzrayim* are likely hidden. There really seems nothing more that stands in our way as we try to find answers to some of the questions that we posed earlier.

In this section we will make a beginning. In the final section we will bring this exciting exploratory trip to a conclusion.

Let us take a careful look at the first section of BeChukosai.*

1. If you will follow My decrees and observe My commandments and perform them.
2. Then I will provide your rains in their time, and the land will give its produce and the trees of the field will give its fruit. Your threshing will last until the grape harvest, and the grape harvest will last until the sowing; you will have your fill of food and you will dwell securely in your land. I will grant peace in the land, and you will

---

* I quoted the entire piece because context matters. Please be aware that the spaces that I left between the various sections are entirely artificial. I decided to insert them simply in order to make the identification of the different sections that I plan to discuss more readily accomplished. Let's agree that I will call them sections 1, 2, 3, and 4 respectively.

sleep without fear; I will rid the land of wild animals and the sword will not pass through the land. You will chase away your enemies and they will fall before your sword. Five of you will chase away one hundred, and a hundred of you will chase away ten thousand; and your enemies will fall before you by the sword.

3. I will place My Sanctuary among you; and My spirit will not reject you. I will walk among you, I will be God unto you and you will be a people unto Me.

4. I am HaShem Your God, who took you out of the land of Egypt from being their slaves; I broke the pegs of your yoke and I led you with your head held high.*

It seems to me that sections 2 and 3 are self-explanatory. God promises that if we do what we are called upon to do 1.), everything will turn out for the very best. Both the physical aspects of our lives 2.) and our spiritual needs 3.) will be granted us in abundance.

What about section 4? That is where we really need to head. For the moment, though, we are going to have to curb our impatience. I promise that the wait will turn out to have been worthwhile. It is really what we have been waiting for throughout these last four chapters. It will provide a glorious finale to our search for the authentic Pesach.

In the meantime, logic demands that we start with section 1.

The Ribono shel Olam is saying something like this: "Look. We have reached a point at which I have fulfilled everything that I promised the Forefathers, excepting only that I have not yet returned you to Eretz Yisrael. I am about to fulfill this promise, too. It will only be a couple more days.** But we have to do it right. We do not want any misunderstandings. In one short sentence, I will tell you what will be required of you if it is to work. After all that you have been through these last cou-

---

* I have borrowed heavily from R. Aryeh Kaplan's *The Living Torah* for the rendering of this passage.

** Who, at this time, could possibly have foreseen the dreadful aberration of the spies? If only, if only....We had everything in our hands and we let it slip out of our grasp.

ple of years, you should not find these demands too difficult.* But you must know that I am deadly serious. Very shortly you will hear what lies in store for you if you do not live up to your responsibilities. Privilege *always* comes wrapped in responsibility.

"Please, please listen carefully!"

What conditions is the Ribono shel Olam laying down? What is section 1 telling us about ourselves and the Ribono shel Olam? What is going to make that relationship prosper?[4]

I think it best to introduce our discussion with the following quote from Letter 3 in the first volume of the *Igros Chazon Ish.*

> The Torah is not designed to teach us superficiality in the way we run our lives. After all, Chazal teach us that Torah will not meaningfully affect anybody who does not sacrifice his very life for its truths. The "death" contemplated here is the determination to part ways with superficiality and to make one's spiritual home in the land of "deep" living, where one succeeds in penetrating to even the "depths within the depths" of life.
>
> The secret of living in the paths that Torah lays out for us is to ruthlessly annihilate surface living. Heroism can flourish only when the unheroic has been jettisoned. Smash the egotistical tendencies that constitute the life of the untaught, the untrained, nature, and you will have embarked upon the right path.

It is for this reason that at the very beginning of BeChukosai Rashi, based on Chazal, points out to us that learning Torah without enormous exertions is not what is required. *You are called upon to labor strenuously in your learning.* Maharal (Gur Aryeh there) explains that Chazal derive this principle from

---

* Within the next few sentences we are going to see that we will be expected to live as would befit a people whose ethos is based upon the world to come rather than being denizens in good standing in this world. The life in the desert that *klal Yisrael* had lived since leaving Egypt would, certainly should, have been an excellent preparation.

the fact that the Torah uses the metaphor of *walking* in its description of learning.* Here is a small quote: *This is derived from the fact that the Torah uses the metaphor of walking.* This can be understood in one of two ways. Either since walking is a tiring activity, it can serve well as a metaphor for the type of learning that is required. Or, because when walking, we constantly move on to a new place, that can remind us of the need never to rest on our laurels. There will always be new depths to discover, more aspects of the case to be explored.

Learning Torah is heavy work indeed.

Clearly there appears to be a serious, perhaps unbridgeable, disconnect between the Torah and ordinary, otherwise quite innocent, life in this, our beautiful world.[5]

Why is that so? Why, if this is the place where the Ribono shel Olam wants us to be, should life as it is lived here to the fullest be incompatible with the most basic of our spiritual needs? Here is a phrase that the Maharal uses as he makes his case: *Because the body is in opposition to the mind.* We humans, or at least we Jews, seem to strike the only jarring note in an otherwise perfectly balanced world. Polar bears and mosquitoes, as well as all the other myriads of organisms of which they may be considered representative, are doing just fine; they do not experience any clashes between their bodies and what passes for their minds. Why do just we have to be the complicating factor?

The answer to this is contained in the previous chapter. We do not belong here. We are aliens, at best visitors, having been placed here not by right but on sufferance. For us, living with a physical body is not a natural but an acquired skill. We are never quite at home and the fit is never perfect.

*   *   *

We are finally ready to approach section 4, the verse that I believe to be the repository of the secrets of *yetzi'as Mitzrayim* that till now have eluded me.

Here it is once more.

I am HaShem your God, who took you out of the land of Egypt,

---

* *If you will* WALK IN MY STATUTES...

from being their slaves; I broke the pegs of your yoke and I led you
with your head held high.

Let us savor the almost palpable excitement of the situation. This verse is the absolute end of the *yetzi'as Mitzrayim*
narrative. From here on, that "delivery-room drama" fades
into history, and we move on to our toddler stage, the account of our experience in the desert. The closing sentence
is the one that we remember best; it is the snapshot that we
are meant to carry around in our mental wallet. *Komemiyus*,
standing erect, with its intimations of majesty and the power
of its uniqueness,* is the code word chosen by the Ribono shel
Olam that, as the centuries pass, will continue to open the
combination locks that permit us access to our memory gates.

What are we being told?

Graphic contrast will be our friend. Check out this
diagram.

BECHUKOSAI	VA'EIRA
I will rest My Spirit among you.	1. I will bring you out from under the burden that Egypt imposes on you.
4. You will be a nation [dedicated] to Me.	2. And free you from their slavery
2. and 3. I broke the pegs of your yoke.	3. I will liberate you with a demonstration of My power and with great acts of judgment.
1. And led you forth with your heads held high.	4. And I will take you to Myself as a nation…

[Please understand that the parallelisms to VaEira that I
try to indicate in the BeChukosai column are no more than
approximations.

You will have noticed that the first entry in the BeChukosai

---

* Please note that, according to my search program, this is the *only* time in the
entire TaNaCh that this word occurs. That must be telling us something!

column is not numbered. I cannot see that it has a parallel in the earlier *parshah*. This seems to back up those Rishonim who maintain that the need for building a communal Mishkan arose only as a result of the sin of the Golden Calf. Plan A had been that each home would be a mini-Tabernacle with the firstborn serving as the *kohen*.]

The differences between the two passages appear to me to be stupendous. I suppose that this should not come as a surprise. It is true that the time lapse between the two occasions when these pronouncements were made is not very large, but much has happened. It has been a roller-coaster ride from unimaginable heights (splitting of the Red Sea, receiving the Torah at Mount Sinai) to the pathetic whimpering of *Is HaShem in our midst, or not?* and the rowdy abandon of the "calf dances."

It has been a maturing experience and things must have changed very much.

Let us analyze.

What I am about to suggest is the result of my own thinking. I am not quoting from any book. Please use your own judgment or seek guidance as to whether or not what I am suggesting is acceptable.

It seems to me that the earlier passage relates to the latter one as body relates to soul, as doing relates to being. Here is how:

The earlier passage addresses a slave people in the language that, after two hundred years of unremitting labor, they would likely understand. It concentrates upon what would matter to them at that stage of their lives. It sounds something like this: "For as long as you remember you have been made to bear unbearable burdens. That is going to change. I will remove you from the clutches of those who, for so long, have lorded it over you (1). Not only will they no longer be able to make you work (2), you will also be able to witness the well-deserved punishments with which I intend to afflict them (3). But that is not all. When all this is done, you will become My very special nation (4).

In all this there is absolutely no mention of any anticipated change in the people *as* people. If we had only this passage, we might have supposed that after *yetzi'as Mitzrayim* they were to remain exactly what they had been before. They would be a "slave people" with no slavery to perform. What difference there was would be expressed only in the fact that nobody would be able to make them get out of bed in the morning.

The later passage projects an entirely different picture. It is much shorter than the other one but, saying less, it says much, much more. It defines *yetzi'as Mitzrayim* as a fundamental change in the posture of the people. From being crushed and bent beneath the heavy yoke of servitude,[6] they would now stand up straight—uncontrolled, but, more important, unbowed.*

Let us explore this concept. Why is "unbowed" important?

In the footnote below, we learned that Rashi explains *komemiyus* as *an erect posture.*[7] What is so great about erect postures?

I would suggest that, in the eyes of Chazal, it is the perfect antipode to servitude. The laws governing the *eved Ivri* can illustrate the implications of being a servant very vividly, thus allowing us to draw conclusions concerning the character of its opposite, the *one who stands erect.*

I have dealt with this topic at length in my book *I Brought You Unto Me* (on the Ten Commandments), which I published in 2008. Here are a few paragraphs; if you have access to that book, you might enjoy reading and thinking about the entire piece (in chapter 20).

> The institution of *eved Ivri* is one that to American sensibilities (perhaps too, our own) seems crude and primitive. To sell a person into slavery in order to pay off a debt!? How dreadful and barbaric! So much for American sensibilities! The fact is, of course, that it projects exquisite sensitivity and, when we think about it, evidences the love and concern that the Ribono shel Olam has for even His erring sons.

---

* On the word *komemiyus*, Rashi comments, *In an erect posture.*

Let us quickly rehearse some of the salient features of this institution. In the first place, the sale must take place in private. It is forbidden to sell the thief in the slave market or to stand him up on a platform to show off his advantages to best effect. Once he is bought, the first thing that the new master learns is that for the next six years he will have to feed and clothe the family of his new *eved*. No matter how many children the *eved* has, they all now become the master's responsibility.

The work that the master can demand from his *eved* is strictly limited to activities that will not offend against his dignity...

And so on. The shock comes a few paragraphs later.

Beautiful! Is it not? And yet, suddenly without warning, this heartwarming picture comes crashing down all around us. Our idyllic picture explodes in our faces and we are crushed and broken by what the Torah prescribes for this *eved*. His owner has the right to make him cohabit with a non-Jewish slave girl, in order that children born of that union will, by halachic fiat, be slaves to the owner. Jewish men are forbidden to cohabit with such women, Jewish women are forbidden to cohabit with men who have the same status. And here we have this *eved* forced to do what in other circumstances would have been strictly interdicted for him. We are telling him, "Your Jewishness is somehow tainted. What for others is unthinkable, for you is not only permitted but obligatory. When you stole, you traded in some of your *Yiddishkeit*. Go where they are sending you. Spend your nights with the real slaves. Till your years of servitude are up, that is where you belong!"

Can there be a greater horror? Can there be a greater shame?

For a discussion of some of the implications of this puzzling *halachah* you are going to have to go to that other chapter. Here I am more interested in the mechanics that are at play. What is *servitude*, that it can incorporate within itself such apparent contradictions?

I believe that it is a matter of reinterpreting the nature of servitude, to move it from a definition of what a person might be called upon to *do*, to what he might be called upon to *be*. This can best be done by looking in Kiddushin 9a.

> He has done double the work of a hired hand (Devarim 15:18). A hired hand works only by day, but an *eved Ivri* works not only by day, but also by night. But can this be true? Does the Torah not require that "his stay with you should be good"? "With you" implies equality. The food you give him must be every bit as good as that which you yourself eat. [How then can it be countenanced that he should work both by day and by night?] [It does of course not require that he work a double shift. It means that his master can make him cohabit with a Canaanite slave woman.]

The language makes it very clear that cohabiting with the slave woman is not to be considered "work." If, nevertheless, he is forced to do so, it must be that servitude implies a certain state of "being." His status as a full-fledged Jew has undergone a subtle change to the extent that actions that would be forbidden to someone who has not compromised his standing are permitted, and even obligatory, for him. While the obligation to "work" is not a twenty-four-hour proposition, his standing as a servant is.

It is that standing that, in Torah thought, is evoked by the picture of the yoke. It is a malevolent presence. It is alien; above all it is imposed. It is a constant testimony to a compromised humanity. At the moment that the slave's servitude becomes operative, he changes from subject to object. To a debilitating extent he has ceased to be arbiter of his own actions. He is shackled to his master's will.

What happens to us when, relieved of our yokes, we stand erect? What are the implications of the *head held high*, which describes the man whom the Ribono shel Olam had in mind when he took us out of Mitzrayim?

Here is an interesting oxymoron that we must now explore. It contemplates the freedom that is so unfettered that it begets the unbounded joy of an "un-freedom" imposed by unseen shackles that are the more confining because they really do not confine at all.

What does all that mean?

It describes the exhilarating joy of being free of even the cruelest, the most insidious masters of all—the inner demons that so often grind down our most earnestly undertaken resolutions, making sport of our pathetic dreams that we can become masters over ourselves. That greatest of all freedoms can and does build ruthlessly confining walls around us to the end that the "אינך רשאי" of our conscience becomes, almost literally, the "לא תוכל" of the Torah text.*[8]

*   *   *

The time has come to bring this chapter to an end. Earlier we wondered why specifically the term *zeman cheiruseinu*, the time of our freedom, is used to describe Pesach. I introduced the subject with the following:

> Careful now! Does that *zeman cheiruseinu*, time of our freedom, not strike a sour note? Is that what Pesach really is? Is it just a negative, an absence of the onus of slavery, a license to sleep late, a joy at being able to dispose of our time and energies as we are inclined to do? It does seem rather bland, does it not?
>
> We are entering some very tricky territory.
>
> What exactly did *yetzi'as Mitzrayim* do for us?

---

* Reference is to Devarim 12:17, *You will be unable to eat in your gates*, that prohibits certain foods in certain situations. Rashi remarks on *You will be unable* that the act is most certainly physically possible, so you really *can*. The meaning is, *you are not permitted*. The idea of expressing the prohibition by using the root word י כ ל (which speaks of *ability*) is of course to convey the idea that the knowledge that doing this or that would militate against God's will ought to bind our freedom more effectively than would the strongest physical shackles. Give yourself a treat and see endnote 8.

119

I then expanded upon this matter in endnote 2 and suggest that you now take the time to reread (or read) that note. I want to redeem the promise that I made there, that by the end of this chapter we will have found an explanation.

Here are my thoughts on this matter.

A perennial issue with which I have dealt quite often in this series of books concerns the admissibility of comparisons between *lashon hakodesh* and other languages in the way that language tends to develop. If we can pin down certain associations that people tend to make between given words and given, let us say, behaviors, in, for example English, is it legitimate to expect that that same phenomenon might also be detectable in *Lashon HaKodesh*?

Here is an example* of what I mean. We are all familiar with the word *courteous*, which describes a well-mannered, sensitive approach in one's relationship with people. The history of the word appears to be more or less as follows: Kings held "court" in a palace in which the functionaries were not surprisingly known as *courtiers*. Now in the minds of the plebeians (certainly mostly erroneously), this class of people was assumed to be well-mannered and sensitive in their dealings. As a result of this assumption such behavior, even when divorced from any royal context, began to be described as *courteous*. In short, a psychological leap was made between noun and adverb: A courtier acts in a well-mannered and sensitive fashion; therefore anybody, even, let us say, a taxi driver far removed from the court, who acts in this approved manner would still be described as courteous.

Is it legitimate to expect to find—and therefore be likely to find—similar leaps of association in *Lashon HaKodesh*?

In the present instance, and providentially, specifically concerning the use of *cheirus*, we have an example that can throw light on this matter.

Here is a quote from Shabbos 109a.

---

* Taken from C. S. Lewis, *Studies in Words*.

The impurity that attaches to our hands after a night's sleep is a free and independent entity. [It is] a *"bas chorin."* It is no one's slave. [It will not permit itself to be pushed around.] It refuses to depart until the hands are washed three times (*negel wasser*).

You cannot fool around with this impurity. It insists that its demands be met. If it feels that it ought not to depart without the halachically approved ablutions having taken place, it will not budge with less. Well and good. But why express this obstinacy in terms that, in themselves, are manifestly inappropriate here?* Why not use something like *she is most particular?***

If, however, we could suggest that the tendency to project character traits assumed to belong to a certain group of people (in the example that we cited above, the courtier; in our case, *the free*) outward beyond the meaning of the original noun form exists also in *lashon hakodesh*, then there would be no problem in assigning a dictionary meaning to the term *bas chorin* as, *one who acts like a bas chorin.*[9]

Earlier in this chapter we began worrying about the suitability of the expression *cheirus*, "freedom," that assumes such an important role in our celebration of the *yetzi'as Mitzrayim* saga. You might want just to skim those few paragraphs once more to jog your memory. At one point I really did view this issue as a serious issue.

That problem has, at least in my mind, been solved by the various topics that we discussed in this chapter. This fact hit me forcibly when I realized that the *Targum* of *komemiyus* is "with *cheirus*."

---

* The ArtScroll Gemara translates *bas chorin* as *a free spirit*. I respectfully suggest that this takes a liberty with the text that may not be justified. "Free spirit" is an idiom used in English to describe certain character traits. Here is one dictionary definition: *One who is not restrained, as by convention or obligation.* Apart from the fact that this is not precisely what is meant here, we all know that idioms are poor travelers. To assume that the same words translated into Aramaic would yield the same idea seems to me to be too much of a stretch.

** See Bava Kama 87a: *Gavra kapdana hu.*

CHEIRUS IS THE STATE IN WHICH ONE ACTS AS A
BEN CHORIN.

I indicated earlier in this chapter that I believe that the
common translation of *cheirus* as *freedom* is flawed, terribly
and dangerously flawed. It is flawed not because it says something that is not true. It is *a* truth, but not the whole truth.
The idea expressed by the word "freedom" is at the same time
too broad and too narrow. It is too broad because not everyone who is "free" can be said to be a *ben chorin*,* and it is too
narrow because it ignores the very quality that gives *cheirus* its
unique character.

That character is the aristocracy, the very royalty,** which is
implied in *komemiyus*.

Zeman cheiruseinu is not the season of our freedom, but the
season at which we were able to straighten our backs and assume the posture that speaks of an inner mastery as we described it earlier in this chapter. It is the moment when we
entered the ranks of the *sarim, the princes* to whom the Ribono
shel Olam was willing to entrust His Torah.***

I think that we have come to a point at which we can hon-
estly tell ourselves that Pesach has become a little clearer to us
than it was before.

---

* With the best will in the world, not every free person can be described as
having an aristocratic bearing.
** See Radak to I Kings 21:8 on *Cheirim*. He equates them with various levels
of aristocracy.
*** See Rashi to *mamleches kohanim* at Shemos 19:6.

PART IV

Succos

11.

The Na'anu'im*

*P*lease listen in on this imagined conversation:

—Why do we shake the *lulav* on Succos?

—I think it has something to do with holding back evil spirits,** the same kind of things that we hold at bay every morning by washing *negel wasser*.

—Is there any particular reason why we are worried about these evil spirits more on Succos than at any other time?

—I don't know.

—Do you find the "shaking ceremony" particularly meaningful? Does it "shake you up" spiritually? Does it make you feel connected to the Ribono shel Olam in a way that is at least somewhat comparable to the *avodah* on Yom Kippur?

—Yes. It does, kind of. I look around and see that everybody invests the procedure with a lot of *kavanah*, so I do, too. But, to tell the truth, I can't really tell you why. I certainly don't have the equivalent feeling when I wash

---

* This is the Hebrew term for *moving things around* or *shaking them*. It is commonly used to describe the "shaking" of the *lulav* and *esrog* that is a familiar, and as we shall soon see, central part of our *davening* on Succos.

** The error that our friend is making can (perhaps) be excused. He is perfectly right that the words *Ru'ach Raah* that play a significant role in understanding our *na'anu'im* as we shall soon see below, *can* and in fact *do* refer to *evil spirits* in the context of the discussions of *negel wasser* at the beginning of our Shulchan Aruch. His problem lies in a lack of sophistication in the way language is used. He does not realize that, depending on the context, the same words can mean different things. We shall see in a few moments that, where our *na'anu'im* are concerned, the word "*Ru'ach*" can describe either *direction* (one of the four cardinal compass points) or *wind*. Please see the next footnote.

negel wasser in the morning. The daily victory over those evil spirits that takes place at the sink does not seem to give me the same kind of high as I get when I zap them with my *lulav*. I don't really know what exactly I am supposed to be doing or what I ought to be feeling or, at least thinking. But all in all, it gives me a wonderful feeling. Succos is a great Yom Tov!

—Please understand that I certainly don't want to intrude. But do you mind sharing with me some indication of what you are thinking while you are shaking the *lulav*?

—I suppose I have some vague sense of doing some kind of *teshuvah*. It's a sort of residue from Yom Kippur. Mainly I concentrate on not poking out the eyes of the guy behind me."

Can we do better than this?

Yes we can. But we will not be able to do so until we get our translations* straight.[1] *Ruchos ra'os* in the present context are not *evil spirits* but *harmful winds*.** We are going to have to remember that Succos coincides with the bringing in of the harvest.*** The people's thoughts would naturally turn to the coming year's crop. They prayed that the climatic conditions would favor their efforts at coaxing food from the ground and that the winds upon which they would depend would be benign.

Let us look at the relevant *sugia* (Succah 37b) and see whether we can give some tangible heft to these assertions.

---

* We must be alert to the fact that a single word may often, in different contexts, have different meanings. The Gemara from Succah 37b that we are about to quote revolves about just this issue. Is *"ru'ach"* to be understood as a *compass point* or as *wind*? This is a fact of life of which we must be aware if we are to avoid significant errors. We really need to be very careful.

** In our *sugia*, the expression "bad *ruchos*" is, as we shall soon see, twinned with "bad *telalim* (kinds of dew)." In an agricultural context (see below). wind and dew form a logical twosome.

*** See VaYikra 23:39: *You shall celebrate Succos on the fifteenth day of the seventh month when you* GATHER IN *the produce of the land.*

[Everybody agrees that the *arba minim*, the four species, are to be waved toward north, south, east and west, the four cardinal points of the compass and then upwards and downward. Two opinions are expressed concerning the meaning of these gestures.]

R. Yochanan opines that these gestures indicate the range of the Ribono shel Olam's mastery over all existence. By the gestures that we perform towards the cardinal points, we are testifying that our service is directed to the Ribono shel Olam Whose mastery extends to every direction, and by the upwards and downwards strokes we are testifying that that same God is also master over both heaven and earth.

The tradition passed down from R. Yose bar Chaninah is that the four sideway movements have the task of bringing protection from harmful winds, while the up and down strokes are designed to prevent harmful dew.

I am hoping that you have kept up with the various footnotes and endnotes so that we can move on now to a consideration of how all the hopes and supplications that we harbor in our hearts on Succos may be nudged towards fulfillment through the *avodah* of our *na'anu'im*.

What might be the significance of the particular form that these gestures are to take?*

See the footnote below. I suppose that it could be argued that if Rashi did not find it necessary to comment, we, too, would be well advised to keep silent. Still, I personally have found the following approach to the *na'anu'im* meaningful and inspiring, and think that you might feel the same way. Certainly, as far as I am able to ascertain, there is no reason to eschew additional layers of meaning beyond those that Rashi seems to have taken for granted.

---

* Rashi makes no attempt to explain how these various gestures are supposed to do their job. He seems to feel that what happens is self-explanatory. I think that it is possible to suggest some ideas that can take the whole matter somewhat further.

Hashanah.] It can be compared to two litigants that argued their case in front of a judge. Nobody knows who
won the case. There is a sign that the observers will be
able to read: The one who comes out of the courtroom
carrying the "victory palm frond"[2] will be the one who
won the case.

We, too, had our litigation on Rosh Hashanah. Our
supremacy as God's chosen people was challenged by the
nations of the world. We do not know who won! But on
Succos it all becomes clear. When we rejoice with our
"victory palm frond" and our *esrog,* it becomes clear that
we were the winners.

Well and good. The criterion for knowing who won the
case is for that litigant to, hold the "victory palm frond." So it
is the *holding* of the *lulav* that is decisive. There is no mention
of waving here, so understanding what that ceremony is all
about will require an additional step. Earlier in this chapter
we have already touched upon this issue.*

But here we stumble across a problem. It is of no great interest to us to discover why the Greeks and Romans considered the palm frond to be an appropriate mark of honor for
their conquering athletes. But it is vitally important for us to
understand why waving just these *arba minim* should be effective in bringing about the ends that R. Yochanan and R. Yose
bar Chaninah, respectively, considered desirable.

We will consider this in two steps. In the first step we will
try to become acquainted with what may be the inner significance of these four *minim,* and in the second one we will try
to understand what precisely it is that we are doing when we
wave them in the six directions that the *halachah* specifies.

The *arba minim:* Here are two midrashim taken from the
Yalkut Shimoni.**

---

* Please see above for the opinions of R. Yochanan and R. Yose bar Chaninah.
** Please note that there is nothing in the Yalkut that implies that these two
midrashim (among the many others that are mentioned there) belong together
in any way. They do not follow each other directly. My suggestion that they

If my reading of certain midrashim is correct, there is something very special about our well-loved *arba minim*. I say "well-loved" because I have the feeling that, even taken as simple "mitzvah objects" without at all entering into the hows and whys of the performance of the mitzvah, there appears to be a special delight tied to their acquisition. All serious Jews will take great care that the matzos or the *mezuzos* or the *shofaros* that they buy should meet the highest possible standards. But, that said, we still know that there is nothing quite like buying that one, that perfect, that totally satisfying *lulav* or *esrog*. Why is that so?

That, of course, is easy enough to answer. The requirement that any "mitzvah object" be as beautiful as possible (*hidur* mitzvah) is jacked up several notches in the case of the *arba minim*. From being simply something a little special, the kind of gesture that in English we might describe as a "special touch," it takes on the form of a measurable halachic requirement. Physical beauty is an active ingredient in the performance of the *na'anu'im*, more so than is the case in any other mitzvah.

Why should this be so? I have a suggestion to make. I would like to share it with you.

Here are some midrashim quoted from the Yalkut Shimoni to *parshas* Emor.*

[R. Avin offers an explanation for the fact that the mitzvah of *arba minim* follows so closely upon Rosh

* In the course of this presentation I intend to create a kind of potpourri of midrashim, that is, that I will combine the three midrashim that I am about to quote and suggest that, at least for myself, this mental combination succeeded in making the *na'anu'im* into a particularly inspiring experience. The purpose of this footnote is to inform you, dear reader, that this combination exists only in my mind. In the sources (I used the Yalkut Shimoni) they appear as separate entities with, to the best of my knowledge, no indication that they in any way belong together.

Now, there is nothing wrong with thinking of these three truths together, and I am very happy that the combination occurred to me. Still, it is important to know that the combination *as* combination is, to the best of my knowledge, not mentioned in Chazal.

R. Akiva quotes four verses in which it appears that each of the four species can serve as a metaphor for the Ribono shel Olam. Effectively, when we hold the *arba minim* in our hands, we hold four symbols that, if we use our heads, will bring the Ribono shel Olam to mind.

And then, a little further along:

This is the well-known midrash that finds each of the four species as hinting at a significant body part. The *esrog* is the heart; the *lulav*, the spine; the *hadasim*, the eyes; and the *aravos*, the lips. Together they represent "man"; in this case, the Jewish people.

Taking these two midrashim together (please see the footnote on page 128), it transpires that each time we hold any of the four *minim*, we have, so to speak, both the Ribono shel Olam, as it were, and *klal Yisrael* in inseparable togetherness in our hands. In our minds we have created a Oneness between the Ribono shel Olam and ourselves, a form, one might perhaps say, of compositeness. Now that may mean different things to different people, but I do not think that I am mistaken when I say that knowledge of this truth can make our *na'anu'im* into a very uplifting experience.

The *na'anu'im*: It will be instructive for us to take a quick glance at some of the ideas that animate Maharal's number system.* Before we begin our analysis of numbers 6 and 7, numbers that we will be using in our exposition, we should note Maharal's statement (*Chidushei Aggados* on Chullin 91b) that, "Each number has a 'nature' of its own." That nature is based upon the way that that number is integrated into our physical world.

In what way is the number six integrated into the physical world as we know it? How are we supposed to read the

---

might be combined in just the way that I am about to suggest within, is just that: my suggestion.

* Most of the information that I will use in this section comes from R. Yehoshua Hartman's *Gur Aryeh HaShalem*, volume 9, page 32 and onward.

messages contained in Torah passages in which the number six seems somehow central? In Maharal's thought it is the cube with its six faces (the four compass points plus "up" and "down") that most accurately stands for the integrity (*sheleimus*) of the physical world. See *Gur Aryeh* to Bereishis 26:34:

[Maharal uses Yitzchak's life to demonstrate that multiplying a number by ten projects that number in its absolute completeness. Ten is the number that brings matters to their most ideal expression.] Yitzchak married at forty (four multiplied to perfection by ten) and bore his children at sixty (six multiplied to perfection by ten). Both four and six express a certain level of perfection even before they are multiplied. Four, standing for the four cardinal points of the compass, expresses the totality of plane directions; six, which adds the two possibilities of upward and downward expresses the higher completion of the three-dimensional cube.

Yitzchak was ready for marriage at forty, but for parenthood he had to wait till sixty.

It is certainly no coincidence that the Ribono shel Olam created the world in *six* days. By the end of that "ur-Friday," the physical world was as perfect as it needed to be.

What does "seven" add to "six"?

The following is a paraphrase of the Maharal in Tif'eres Yisrael, chapter 40.

It adds the concept that, besides its six faces, the cube has a seventh property. There is, at its very center, a nonphysical—really an imagined—point that imbues the entire structure with a spiritual element. If a regular cube can be defined as "a three-dimensional object bounded by six square faces, with three meeting at each vertex," the definition of the "Jewish" cube would read, "A cube is a three-dimensional object bounded by six square faces, with three meeting at each vertex, and an imagined point at its center at which the essential 'God-Presence' that animates and gives meaning to all physicality is lodged."

Please think this over very, very carefully. It is our visa into a world that finds completion and justification not at the point, reached at the end of six days, when everything physical is in place, but on the seventh day when, so to speak, the *neshamah* enters the body.

That should do for us in the present context.

Do you see where I am heading in my attempt to understand the *na'anu'im* a little better? Isn't it all becoming clearer now?

Let us spell it out.

I stand with the *arba minim*, symbolizing the oneness of the Ribono shel Olam with klal Yisrael, in my hand. Conceptually, the point at which I am standing can be viewed as the imagined center of an imagined cube. As I stand there armed with the "victory palm frond" that I am holding, I can view myself at that sacred moment, as being surrounded by six very physical planes. Can I somehow penetrate that self-assured façade? Can I somehow imbue that "absence" with a "presence"?

The holy highlight of holy Succos, the moment that can be viewed as the culmination of the *yerach ha'eisanim*, the *month of ineffable ecstasy* that is (or ideally should be) our Tishrei, finally lies at hand. I will try. I will dare to challenge that seemingly impregnable solidity.

Slowly, tentatively I thrust my *arba minim* outward. I expand the reach of my ostensibly nondimensional space. *Give thanks to HaShem for He is good, His kindness endures forever.* What can be done shall be done! I create a nondimensional dimension. On holy Succos the impossible becomes the reality of our world.

12.

Klapping the Hoshanas

*T*his is it: the last photo in our Tishrei album.

As we leaf back through the gorgeous pages of the album, we are reminded of the many moments of high drama that punctuated those wonderful four weeks. This last picture seems out of place. There we are, *arba minim* laid aside, holding on to a rather bedraggled bundle of *aravos*, and looking as though we were not quite certain what exactly we are called upon to do. Does the ceremony of beating the *aravos* speak to us? If yes, of what? If not, why do it?[1]

It leaves us puzzled. There we are, holding, of all things, a bunch of *aravos*, with a bemused look on our faces. What exactly is the meaning of this final act, this banging of the *aravos*?* ** It seems such a comedown from earlier glories. Are these symbols of absence—no taste, no smell, no Torah, no good deeds, no nothing of anything at all—what is left to us

---

* Please note that our assumptions in this chapter are based on the practice that is laid down for us in the Shulchan Aruch. Rashi to Succah 44b seems not to have known of any banging of the *aravos*. He interprets *chavit* as waving. In his view the *aravos* were to be *waved*, not *beaten*.

** There are varying customs concerning the number of times the *aravos* ought to be banged. I was struck by an interesting expression occurring twice at Succah 44a. The issue under discussion was whether or not one ought to make a *berachah* for banging the *aravos*. The Gemara tells of two instances in which *aravos* were brought to one of the *amora'im*. In each case, *he banged and banged* but made no *berachah*.

I would love to know what specific weight was implied by the repeated *he banged and banged*, as the idiom was used at that time. As we speak today, I would suppose that we ought to render the expression, *he kept on banging away*, implying an almost undisciplined orgy of banging. I am not going to make the mistake of assuming that precisely this was the implication of a doubled word a couple of millennia ago. I imagine that we cannot really know.

What do you think?

from this month of the "mighty ones"*? Has our Tishrei, repository of so many hopes, of such firm determination, of the rosy dreams that whispered to us of some measure of success after so many depressing failings, come down to, of all things, simply banging these somewhat disreputable reminders of our inadequacies?

It is an experience fraught with deep emotional undertones. It is not easy to say good-bye to Tishrei with its wealth of "hands-on" experiences, the *mitzvos* that tore at our hearts and penetrated deep, deep down to where our most precious Jewish sensibilities are lodged. But now the time has come. A few seconds of banging and then back to our ordinary, pedestrian lives. All that will be left to us is the disreputable *"geklappte hoshana"*** and a vague feeling of unease about where to put the thing without messing up the shul. It is a defining moment in our Jewish lives. Cold, drab winter suddenly feels uncomfortably close.

What exactly are we supposed to be feeling as we stand there banging away? Is there a thought that is being expressed? Is there a goal that is being reached?*** Unless the friends and acquaintances with whom I discussed this issue happen to be particularly atypical people, I would suppose that, as they were and as I am, you, my loyal readers, are as perplexed as we. What is the value of a custom about which we understand nothing at all?

Let us see whether by learning and thinking hard we can work out something that might make this farewell to Tishrei more meaningful to us.****

---

* *Yerach haeisanim.* See Melachim I 8:2.

** This is a Yiddish expression meaning, *a banged-up hoshana*. It is used to describe anyone who looks tired, dispirited, and unkempt: "You look (or, I feel) like a..."

*** Somebody suggested that, in as much as we view Hoshana Rabba as a kind of closure to the judgment to which we were exposed during the *Yamim Nora'im*, it is possible that the beaten leaves stand in for our sins. We hope that our sins will be distanced from us even as we distance the *aravas'* leaves from their stalk. It sounds a little bland and forced to me.

**** I do not feel it necessary that my ideas be *the* correct explanation. If I can feel that they, at the very least, provide *a* legitimate approach, that is plenty for

I suggest that the method that holds out the most hope that we may end up with something worthwhile is to isolate the constituent parts of this custom and define them independently. Once we feel more at home with each one of them on its own terms, we will have a better sense of what happens when we combine them.

So what are the constituent parts of our problem? Obviously the fact that the day on which it all happens is Hoshana Rabba is significant. Clearly the seventh day of Succos is somehow special. Then there is the fact that it is the *aravah*, not the *hadas* and not the *lulav*, that is banged.*[2] Clearly there is something special about the *aravah*. Then there is the banging itself. What are we expressing with this apparently bizarre action?

So, here we go.

The Day: Although Pesach and Succos are structured similarly in that they both begin with a day of Yom Tov, which is then followed by several days of Chol HaMo'ed, there is a major difference between them. On Pesach the five days (four, for us Jews who live in the Diaspora) of Chol HaMo'ed are one, indivisible block, while on Succos the six days (five for us Diaspora Jews) are each considered to be a separate Yom Tov.** This exceptional aspect of Succos is also reflected in the *ushpizin*, the very special guests whom we invite nightly into our succahs. Each day has its own guest and, while the details may escape most of us, we can certainly agree that the unique nature of each of those wonderful days can be discovered in the identity of the guest who joins us.

On the seventh day of Succos, it is Dovid HaMelech who opts to spend the day with us. What, we must ask ourselves,

---

me. I would feel that this entire book was worthwhile if what follows would make you feel more in control while engaged in this coming year's beating of the *aravos*.

* Please make sure to look at endnote 2.

** This is reflected by the fact that on Chol HaMo'ed Pesach we recite only a partial Hallel, while on Succos each of the days has its own, full Hallel. (See Orech Chaim, 644 and *Mishnah Berurah* 4).

is the special gift that he brings along to show his appreciation of his hosts?

I am sure that there are many, many *sefarim* that discuss this question. I do not know most of them. The one *sefer* that I merited to learn over the years is the *Sefas Emes*, and, while I cannot and do not claim to have any profound understanding of what he says, I *am* able to translate the words and will share with you what I picked up. I will attempt to compose a picture made up of small snippets taken from different passages, and hope that we will end up with a reasonably accurate image.

Let us look at the following segment first.

> The *aravah* represents those that may be said to have neither taste nor fragrance. What then can be said to be special about them? It is the mouth, the ability to speak; and that is what Judaism is really all about. Remember Yitzchak's words when he was not sure which of his sons was asking to be blessed. "The voice is the voice of Yaakov." The skill of appropriate speech is vested in all of Israel, but particularly in King David. It was he who said (Tehilim 109:4) *I am prayer.*
>
> Now, quite obviously, the prayer of righteous people, those who may be said to have both taste and fragrance, those whose life is filled with good deeds, has advantages over that of the "*aravah*" people. But, on the other hand those latter ones, too, have an advantage. Prayer is *all that they have.* They may be said to be "made of" prayer. Their prayer is particularly sweet in the eyes of the Ribono shel Olam. Remember that the root word of *aravah* (*ayin-reish-beis*) also spells *arev,* which translates as *sweet.*
>
> It is for this reason that the seventh day of Succos, the day dedicated to David who represents the very essence of prayer, is called *Hoshanah Rabba* (which translates as, *the great salvation*) because on this day even the very lowly, those that can be said to possess nothing but *prayer* are saved.

Hoshana Rabba is the day on which all the gates of prayer are opened.

So, our guest Dovid HaMelech lends Hoshana Rabba the character of *the yom tefillah*, the day of prayer. In another segment, *Sefas Emes* points out that among the *arba minim*, the four species that are said to represent different parts of the body, it is the *aravah* that is shaped like the lips. The day and its symbol are a perfect fit. Hoshana Rabba is marked as the day of prayerful speech.

I suppose that had we been asked to identify the preeminent day of prayer in our Jewish calendar, many of us would have chosen Yom Kippur. I imagine that in most places our *Yidden* spend more time in *shul* then, than on Hoshana Rabba. But we would not have been correct. Yom Kippur, for us, bereft as we are of the Beis HaMikdash, is indeed the day of "*teshuvah* prayer," by which I mean *prayer as a function of teshuvah.** But for pure prayer, *prayer for the sake of prayer*, it is to Hoshana Rabba that we must turn.

On Hoshanah Rabba, *tefillah* reigns supreme. Think of the seven circuits that we make around the *bimah*, all the while entreating God for salvation. It is for this reason that the "lip-like" *aravah* holds center stage on that day. The very name *hoshana*, "Please save!" that became attached to it testifies to this centrality.

So why end our prayers by beating up the poor *aravah*? It has rendered us hours of faithful service. It seems to us that it deserves better than such an apparently ignominious fate.

Here is something to shock us. Prayer is served best by ceasing to pray!** Please take a look at this passage from the Zohar (referenced by the *Sefas Emes*).

It has been taught that the best prayer is that which consists not of words but of only tears and unarticulated cries. Such an entreaty will never go unanswered.

---

* See Rabbeinu Yonah, *Sha'arei Teshuvah*, fifteenth *ikar*. See also Rav Hutner's *Pachad Yitzchak* on Yom Kippur for several chapters on this topic.
** In its literal sense. See below.

Words are wonderful and efficient tools but they have their limitations. There are feelings that touch us to the very core but that lie far beyond their range. Language can deal only with such words as stand to its service. It simply gives up when feelings slip beyond its reach. All of us have experienced the beauty of a gorgeous sunset and, when trying to convey something of the feelings that it released in us, were reduced to a "Wow! That was kinda* nice, wasn't it!?"

From a taped *shiur* that I once heard from the late Rav Soloveichik, I learned that Dovid HaMelech himself taught us this lesson. Tehilim 150, the *mizmor* that brings the *sefer* to a close, offers only instrumental music in praise of the Ribono shel Olam.** After one hundred and forty-nine *mizmorim* it appears that he had exhausted the capacity of speech. From now on, silence would be his mode of prayer. *To You, silence is praise* (Tehilim 65:2)! The most meaningful praise that we can offer lies far, far beyond the competence of language.

And so, on the day of the *aravah*, the day of the "sweet lips" (see *Sefas Emes* above), the day on which prayer can and does attain its zenith, we end up beating and discarding the *aravah*. It has brought us as far as it is able. Beyond, there lies a world to which it can gain no entry.[3] For us, that world is, of course, called Shemini Atzeres and Simchas Torah.

Who knows but that our custom to dance on Simchas Torah does not derive from the ideas that we have mooted in this chapter. In Tehilim 150, the *mizmor* that rejects the use of words, dance is listed among the acceptable forms of praise (*besof u'*MACHOL).

Perhaps we have really hit upon something.

* * *

I have two short remarks to make, if I am correct, would lend credence to my suggestion.

---

* Believe it or not, a number of dictionaries recognize "kinda" in the sense that I have used it. I saw one example, "That's kinda funny."

** *Praise Him with the shofar blast* and so on.

1. The beating of the *aravos* was initiated by the prophets (Succah 44a). Why the *nevi'im* rather than the Sanhedrin, which, to the best of my knowledge, are usually the ones to enact new *takanos*?

On the *pasuk Aaron your brother will be your navi* (Shemos 7:1), Rashi remarks that *navi* is a form of *niv sefasayim*, a *speaker*. Apparently the *nevi'im* were considered to be masters of the word. They would indeed be the ones who would be in the ideal position to decree the boundaries within which the power of speech could best be used.

2. In the yeshivos with which I have been associated, Hoshanos are recited after Musaf. According to this arrangement, the beating of the *aravos* follows hard upon the pronouncement *The voice of him who is the bearer of great news announces and says*. I have never been able to see a connection between the two. In the context of my suggestions in this chapter, it may well be the use of *kol*, the sound that is not articulated in words, that serves as an appropriate bridge to the *avodah* of the beating of the *aravos*.

PART V

Mezuzah

13.

Things Are Not Always as They Seem

DOES THE RIBONO SHEL OLAM "NEED" US MORE THAN WE NEED HIM?

*T*he title sounds pretty strange, does it not? Does it touch on heresy? Look, this chapter announces itself as being about the mezuzah. How bad can it be? Trust me a little longer and then make up your mind.

Let us try our hand at understanding Shemos 29:45–46.

I will dwell among the children of Israel and I shall be their God.
> They shall know that I am HaShem, their God, Who took them out of the land of Egypt to dwell among them. I am HaShem their God.

How do we deal with the prefix *lamed* in the word LE*shachni* (לשכני, *to dwell*)? Rashi renders it *on condition that….* The meaning would be, *I emancipated you from Egyptian slavery only on the understanding that you would build a Tabernacle in your midst within which I could dwell.* Ramban objects because, so he claims, there is nowhere else where the prefix *lamed* implies a condition.

Here is Ramban's solution to the problem.

> But Ibn Ezra renders *leshachni* as *in order that I might be able to dwell among them.* He has got it right…This verse lets us in on a great mystery. Without it we would certainly have assumed that God's presence in our midst is meant to benefit us, not to benefit Him. Our verse sets us straight. God, as it were, "needs" to be among us. That is reflected in verses like Yeshayahu 49:3: He said to me, "You are My servant, *Israel in whom I glory.* Or Yehoshua 7:9: When the Canaanites…hear of this they

143

will turn upon us and wipe out our very name from the earth. *What then will You do about Your great name?* There are many verses that convey this impression, such as Tehilim 132:13 and 14, For HaShem has chosen Zion, *He has craved it as His seat. This is My resting place for all time. Here I will dwell for I crave it.*

The *lamed* is to be rendered "for the sake of." The *pasuk* then reads, *So that I will have the possibility of dwelling among them.*

As Ramban reads it, this wording turns our most treasured assumptions on their head. It is not that it is for *our* benefit that the Beis HaMikdash was to be erected. Not at all! It is the Ribono shel Olam who "benefits" from the arrangement! Our title for this chapter is beginning to be a little less shocking, is it not?

So it seems all right to carry on. But, here is a flashing, amber light. Ramban describes Ibn Ezra's insight as a great *mystery* or *secret*. By now, all of us know that the "secrets" with which Ramban often deals are not meant for any of us ordinary folk. In his introduction to his Torah commentary, Ramban makes it very clear that he does not wish us to crash in where we are not invited. We shall, of course, abide by these instructions; we shall make no attempt to plumb any of the depths of these shattering assertions. However, armed with this less than perfectly understood concept, we can start taking a few baby steps toward understanding something of the familiar *mezuzos* that grace our doors.

Let us take a look at Avodah Zarah 11a. I think that, if we learn carefully, we can make this into a life-altering experience. A glance at the following quote will show you that the mezuzah appears in only the third paragraph. So we will be making a short but highly significant detour along the way. Our focus will be on the second and third paragraphs.

[Paragraph 1] Onkelos had converted to Judaism. The Roman emperor was upset and sent a troop of soldiers to bring him back. Onkelos initiated a theological discussion with them with the upshot that the soldiers themselves converted to Judaism.

[Paragraph 2] The emperor sent another group of soldiers. Unperturbed, Onkelos offered to share a piquant little piece of trivia with them. When the emperor traveled at night, palace protocol demanded that the page boys, the lowest in the hierarchy, would carry a torch, lighting the way for the person who was immediately superior to them. This was the system. Those of lower rank would light the way for those above them in the hierarchy. This would be followed up to the very top. The highest official would carry the torch for the emperor.

Onkelos then asked the soldiers for whom the emperor might carry a torch. The answer was that, of course, the emperor would not do this for anyone. There was nobody higher than he; it was ridiculous to assume that he would ever lower himself to serve anybody.

Immediately Onkelos countered with his punch line. When Israel was traveling through the wilderness, it was the Ribono shel Olam Himself who lighted the way for them. Shemos 13:21 teaches, *HaShem went before them, in a pillar of smoke by day, to lead the way; and as a pillar of fire at night, to light the way.*

Impressed, the second troop also converted.

[Paragraph 3] The emperor then sent a third group, ordering that there should be no conversation at all. Obediently, Onkelos said nothing but, as they passed a house with a mezuzah on the door, he touched it with his hands and signaled to the soldiers that he would like to know what this object might be. The soldiers signaled back that they had no idea, but that surely he would be able to enlighten them.

He began to speak. The usual arrangement is that the king lives inside the palace while his servants stand guard outside. We Jews are different. We live safely in our houses, but the Ribono shel Olam guards us on the outside, as it is written, *HaShem shall guard your comings and goings, now and forever.*

They converted.

This is a dangerous piece of Gemara! It makes such interesting and pleasant reading that we tend to take it at face value, without feeling the obligation to dig a little deeper. Well, dig we must. Very clearly, the story cannot stand unsupported on its own two feet.[1] I asked my daughter who is very active in the *kiruv* field whether Onkelos's argument is frequently marshaled to convince people that Judaism has much to offer. She told me that she had never heard it used. That struck me as strange. If it was powerful enough to persuade two regiments of rough Roman soldiers to defy their emperor and become Jewish, why would it not work for people who are already looking for the truth?

So let us dig. What was Onkelos demonstrating to the second group of soldiers by pointing out that God Himself "carried" the torch for His people? What does that show? That God is kind? That God is modest? Why would this persuade a bunch of Roman ruffians to run to the beis hamedrash by way of the *mohel* and the *mikveh*?

We are going to have to read between the lines.

Maharal in *Chidushei Aggados Avodah Zarah* discusses some of these issues. Here is what he says to explain God lighting our way through the darkness in the wilderness.

> God needs Israel (?!!!). It is unthinkable that He would even "exist" (?!!!) if there were no Israel. Now whoever needs another depends upon him and, since he needs him, serves him. It follows logically that the Ribono shel Olam would serve Israel.

Recall that we were hesitant about printing the Ramban with which we began this chapter. What about this Maharal! We must tread very carefully here.

It turns out that our understanding of Onkelos's arguments was in error. We had thought that he was demonstrating God's sterling *qualities* (kindness, modesty, and so on). Nothing of the sort! He was defining the relationship within which the Ribono shel Olam and *klal Yisrael* function. This concept needs explaining. We will get to that explanation in good time, but first it makes sense to see what Maharal does with Onkelos's third victory, the one based upon the lessons that can be learned from the mezuzah. We shall find that the second and third arguments are related to each other.

Here are Maharal's ideas as they appear in *Nesivos Olam, Nesiv HaAvodah*, 15:

> The mitzvah of mezuzah requires that the two *parshios*, "Shema" and "VeHayah im Shamo'a," be inscribed upon our doorposts. Each speaks of subjugating ourselves to a yoke. The first is the "yoke of God's kingship"; the second, the "yoke of His commandments."
>
> Our willingness to shoulder these yokes "obliges" God to fill the role with which we have "invested" Him. To the extent that we have made Him our king, he will act as kings are meant to act. A primary duty of a king is to protect his people from their enemies.[2] Once we have absorbed the message of the mezuzah, that the Ribono shel Olam is our king and that we are bound to fulfill His commandments, He will certainly make sure that no harm befalls us. It is in this sense that the mezuzah protects our homes.

Once more we have the Ribono shel Olam "serving" His people by protecting them. In the first instance it was a matter of guiding them through the dark as they made their way through the wilderness. In the case of the mezuzah He keeps us safe in our homes. Unsurprisingly, the principles are related. Somehow the Ribono shel Olam "needs" us. He is "dependent" upon us and therefore "serves" us.

Can we have some idea of what this all means?

There must be hundreds of references in the Maharal upon which I might be able to base the idea that I am about to spell out. I would not know where to look for them but I happened to come across the one that I am about to quote and I think it will satisfy.

The Maharal that I found discusses Rashi's assertion (at Shemos 3:2) that the Ribono shel Olam appeared to Moshe Rabbeinu from within the thornbush because, apparently, we and He "share" a single fate.* Studied superficially, it might have been supposed that Chazal meant that the Ribono shel Olam wished to suffer along with His beloved *Yidden*. Maharal puts short shrift to this idea.

See the footnote below. The sense of this verse is not at all that God is in any kind of trouble. Far be it from us to maintain any such idea. Rather, the meaning is that the Ribono shel Olam is "shackled" to us and is therefore, in all circumstances in which we find ourselves, "with" us. It follows that when we are in trouble, God's kingship cannot be said to be "complete." God chose to appear to Moshe Rabbeinu from within the thornbush because, at that moment, His kingship was less than perfect.

Having said all this, it still must be understood that all this must be understood in only a relative sense. Relative to us, denizens as we are in our physical world, it can be said that when we are in trouble, God's kingship is somehow lacking something. But God, as He really "is" in an absolute sense, can by definition never lack anything at all.

This really appears to be the key to understanding all those ideas that shocked us so much in the last few paragraphs. How, we wondered, are we to make sense of expressions that convey the idea that the Ribono shel Olam "needs" us, is "dependent" on us, and consequently is "bound" to "serve" us? It sounds sacrilegious, does it not?

This short Maharal makes everything clear. Of course we are not discussing the Ribono shel Olam *as* the Ribono shel Olam, in His essence. As He really is, nothing is lacking, no needs can bind Him, no dependence of any kind can limit his scope. Whatever Maharal taught, whatever dynamic he de-

* This is based on Tehilim 91:15 where the Ribono shel Olam asserts that, *I am with them in their troubles.*

tected in the functioning of the pillar of fire and the mezuzah, applied only to God's presence in this, our physical world. Here, His very perfection makes him "imperfect." He cannot be grasped by our puny senses that are designed for interaction with lesser phenomena. And yet...and yet, He so much longs to be a presence here. I will quote myself from chapter 19 of my book on Tish'ah Be'Av and the *Meraglim*:

> Let us examine to what extent the idea of "wanting" anything is applicable to the Ribono Shel Olam, the Omnipotent.
>
> A good place to consider is BeMidbar Rabba 10.
>
> שוקיו (*Shokav*) (in Shir HaShirim 5:15, lit. "His thighs") can hint at שקק (*shokak*), "to crave." Thus, the word refers to...this world, which God craved, as it is written, *His craving is centered upon me* (Shir HaShirim 7:11).

Apparently, there is one thing that even an omnipotent God lacks. He lacks the *voluntary* obeisance with which a creature, full of love and awe, turns to its Creator. A cosmos infinitely full of infinite possibilities nevertheless lacks that one, infinitely important, element. For that, God needs puny, fallible, imperfect man. There is no way around that. God longs for man because only man can provide the one thing that omnipotence cannot deliver.

Our wholehearted services, freely offered in love and submission, is the one thing, by definition the only thing, that the Ribono Shel Olam can "want" from us. Without us He cannot have it.

There is only one way around this difficulty. If man, the denizen of this, our physical world, is to be able to find a relationship with the Ribono shel Olam, it will be in and through *klal Yisrael*. Here we have the acme of "need" and "dependence" even as these apparently totally inappropriate words must be applied to the Ribono shel Olam. His goodness, His determination that every man be given the possibility to get to know Him, opens Him up to "vulnerability." God Himself shoulders the "servitude" of looking after Israel's needs. It must be done and so it shall be done.

We have now come to a point at which we can unravel the two issues that, earlier in this chapter, we left dangling.

One concerned Onkelos's arguments from the pillar of fire and the mezuzah. A simple reading of the passage seemed to indicate that he was demonstrating the Ribono shel Olam's kindness. However, we felt that this alone could not possibly have persuaded the soldiers to convert. Why should they? Based on Maharal, we therefore posited that he was defining the relationship within which the Ribono shel Olam and *klal Yisrael* function. We promised that this would become clear later in this chapter. We have now fulfilled that promise. We have learned that, in our physical world, the Ribono shel Olam "must" subordinate Himself to *klal Yisrael*. He "stands in need of them" and therefore is willing to "serve" them. We can understand why the soldiers would have wanted to throw in their lot with such a nation.

We were also puzzled by the fact that the Onkelos story did not seem to figure prominently on the "*kiruv* circuit" that is such a wonderful and important part of today's Jewish society. With tongue firmly in cheek (see endnote 1), we mused that if the story managed to persuade hardened Roman soldiers for whom the idea of converting had been completely off the screen, it would certainly resonate with the thoughtful and searching crowd at the weekend seminar.

Now that we have discovered that the point of the story was not the kindness of the Ribono shel Olam but the significance of *klal Yisrael's* standing in our stupendous but oh so needy world, the answer is obvious. Onkelos's magic is of course the heart and energy of every *kiruv* seminar. The wrapping in which we deliver this essential message is a matter of taste, and different generations have different predilections, but the essence is the same.

* * *

It is beginning to look as though the mezuzah can be the key to understanding the difficult Ramban with which we started this chapter. We see now that *leshachni besocham, to dwell in their midst,* is firmly anchored in the mitzvah of mezuzah.

Up to this point we have met the mezuzah as a symbol of God's interest in the safety of our homes. He "stands guard" at our door to protect us from all evil.* In the following chapter we will analyze this concept a little further.

---

* It seems appropriate at this point to quote a line from the *Aruch HaShulchan,* Yoreh De'ah 285:3. After having devoted paragraph 2 to discussing other aspects of the mezuzah, aspects to which we will devote the next chapter, he writes: *And aside from this, the house is protected through it...but in any case, the sole intention for the fulfillment of the* mitzvah *should be for the sake of fulfilling HaShem's commands, and the reward will come on its own.*

14.

Burrowing Into the Woodwork

*W*ell, that was quite a chapter, was it not? It took us a while to get used to the idea of the Ribono shel Olam "feeling Himself obliged" to "stand sentry" at our front doors. Still, I have the feeling that by the end of the chapter we all began to feel comfortable with the ideas that we worked out there. However, we are left with some uncertainties. Who is doing the guarding? Is it the Ribono shel Olam Himself or is it the mezuzah? If it is the Ribono shel Olam, what precisely is the function of the piece of parchment (mezuzah) nailed to the doorpost? If it is the mezuzah, how do we understand the language that Onkelos used? He seemed to pull no punches at all. In his view it is the king himself who is standing outside making the house safe for his subjects.

We will devote this chapter to trying to solve this conundrum.

When we think about the mezuzah we should do so together with tefillin and tzitzis since Chazal bundle them together when they speak of the foursome of *"mal'achim"* that accompanies us, guarding us from sin. Here is Rambam's language in *Hilchos Tefillin* 6:13. Our *Chachamim* taught us that whoever has tefillin on his head and arm, tzitzis on his garment, and a mezuzah on his door can be assumed to be free of sin. This, because he has a slew of guards who remind him [to maintain his standards]. These [four] are the "angels" that save him from sinning, as it is written, *The angel of God is always with those who fear Him, to keep him from harm.*

I think it would be a good idea to examine the language that the Torah and the Rambam use when speaking of these four.

RAMBAM, MISHNEH TORAH	RAMBAM, SEFER HAMITZVOS	TORAH TEXT	
To tie them on the arm.	We are commanded to *place* tefillin on our arm.	"You shall tie them as a sign on your arm.	The tefillin that are worn on the arm.
The tefillin shall be *on* the head.	We are commanded to *place* tefillin on our head.	"They shall function as an ornament between your eyes.	The tefillin that are worn on the head.
"To make tzitzis on the corners of a garment."	That we are commanded to make tzitzis.	"And you shall make for them tzitzis.	Tzitzis
To fix a mezuzah on the entrances of the houses.	To make *mezuzos.*	You shall write them on the *mezuzos* (doorposts) of your home.	Mezuzah

I suggest that it is relatively easy to understand the system that the Rambam uses in the first three. The fourth, the mezuzah, needs more careful analysis.

Here is how.

In the case of the two tefillin the Torah is, to a certain degree, specific. It wants us to "tie" the *shel yad* on our arms and to "have" the *shel rosh* in the specified position.[1] In the *Sefer HaMitzvos* the Rambam eliminates the details. He uses the term *lehaniach, to place** for both. He is only interested in enumerating the *mitzvos* in general terms. In the *Yad*, as is appropriate, he reverts to the details.

Rambam's presentation of tzitzis is, as far as I can see, logical and consistent. The Torah uses *asah* (*ve'ASU lahem* tzitzis) and the Rambam sticks with that.**

Against all expectations, Rambam in the *Sefer HaMitzvos* uses the same root word (*asah*), to make, for the mezuzah. I believe it to be unexpected because the Torah uses the form of *to write* (*kasav*), and Rambam in the *Mishneh Torah* uses *to fix* (*kava*). So why use this form of "*making*" mezuzos?

The problem is more serious than it sounds. Please look at second footnote below where you will find that in the *parshah* of tzitzis the root word "to make" (*asah*) refers to the creation of the "branch" at each corner. In that context the use of the word is absolutely appropriate. A number of technical details are involved: making the hole in the right place, threading the strings through the hole, knotting them, and so on.*** However, that creative activity has no parallel in the case of the mezuzah. By the time the owner of the house nails the parchment to the doorpost, the mezuzah has already been written and nothing is left to do but to fix it there. The term can also not refer to the writing of the text since, as far as I can gather, that is not a part of the mitzvah. So what can the phrase, *to make the* mezuzah, possibly mean?

I have a suggestion, but in order to get to that we are going

---

* His choice is presumably based on the wording of the *berachah* "lehaniach tefillin."

** As far as I can see, Rambam maintains that consistency in the actual *halachos*. See 1:1, 1:5, and elsewhere. My search engine found twenty-eight uses of *asah* in *Hilchos Tzitzis*. We will discuss the precise meaning of *asah* as used here, later when we think about the same root word in connection with the mezuzah (where Rambam uses it in the *Sefer HaMitzvos*). Here it seems to describe the act of creating the *anaf* (literally, "branch"), the expression that Rambam uses to describe the *tzitzios* with all their components (stem, knots, and so on) that hang from each of the corners.

*** Whether or not we would use ע ש ה today is entirely irrelevant. In this series of books we have noted again and again that language is alive and dynamic; nuance and even meaning can change radically over the centuries.

to have to study the Torah text in which the mitzvah of mezuzah is presented.

Let us remember that the base meaning of mezuzah is *doorpost*.* One would suppose that the words, *And you shall write them on the mezuzos of your house,* can only mean, *Write them** on the doorpost of the house.* Quite clearly, it seems that the actual words are to be written on the actual doorposts; nothing is said about writing them on a piece of parchment that is then to be nailed there. The issue is discussed at Menachos 34a (near the bottom of the page) and the details need not concern us here. However, a careful examination of that passage convinces me that the reading of the text on which the Gemara bases its conclusions is based not upon the literal meaning of the words (*peshat*) but on an interpretive examination of the entire text (*derash*). The simple meaning of the *pasuk* does not change. We all know that *the literal meaning is never discarded and must also have been chosen because it has something of significance to teach us* (Shabbos 63a), so, even after that *sugia* we have our work cut out for us. We need to find an explanation for the strange wording.

Then there is the linguistic puzzle. Why call the piece of parchment upon which the two *parshiyos* are written a "doorpost"*** (mezuzah)? Surely it does not become a "doorpost" because it is affixed to one. After all, we do not call our tefillin "*arm*" or "*head.*"

Some really big things seem to be happening here. Let us not miss out on them!

Let us spell out what our analysis has yielded thus far.

The designated *parshiyos* are written on a parchment and it is that which is attached to the doorpost. But, apparently, that is no more than a technical necessity. Once attached to the doorpost it is considered, for practical purposes, to be written directly *on* the doorpost. The message is melded onto, indeed

---

* Remember that the blood of the Pesach had to be smeared upon the lintel and the *mezuzos,* the two doorposts.

** This must refer to the *devarim* (matters) mentioned earlier in the *parshah.*

*** The use is already attested in the Mishnah (Menachos 3:7). The usage is an ancient one.

into, the doorpost (*mezuzah*) and therefore itself becomes [a part of] it![2] It has, so to speak, earned the name mezuzah.

This thought can be taken further. What I am about to suggest should not be looked upon as another, unconnected, explanation. If what I have just written is the "body" of my theory, what follows stands in for the soul.

Here is an excerpt taken from R. Samson Raphael Hirsch's Shemos commentary.

> The doorposts and the lintel represent the entire house. The concept of "home" comprises two elements: it is a social insulation vis-à-vis society and provides physical insulation against the forces of nature. The first is signified by the two doorposts (mezuzos—from the root zuz, "to move") that control the flow of those who enter and exit, representing the walls which form a social barrier...

If it is true that the door posts/walls of the house control the social ambience of the home, then it is certainly true that the roll of parchment affixed to those doorposts, proclaiming that in this house *the acceptance of the yoke of Heaven and the yoke of mitzvos* reign supreme, shares directly in that task. It, itself, becomes an integral part of the doorpost. (In effect it becomes a mezuzah!) Unambiguously, it announces who is to be welcome in this house and who is to be excluded. The *Chachamim* knew what they were doing when they proclaimed the mezuzah to be a "mezuzah" (doorpost).

The mezuzah, as it were, burrows into the woodwork of the doorpost and blends into it; hence it becomes a part of the doorpost and shares its name. Its message is beamed inward; it turns the home into an incubator that lays the groundwork for a successful encounter with the outside world.

Have we come any nearer than we were earlier to a solution of the seemingly strange expression that the Torah uses when it tells us to *write these things on* the doorposts? It does not seem so. Although we have discovered—and a great discovery it is—that once the mezuzah has been affixed it becomes an integral part of the doorpost, does that mean that when I am *writing* the mezuzah it is upon the doorpost that I am doing so? The idea does not sit well with me. So why would the Ribono shel Olam write His Torah in a way that requires a leap of faith to understand it?

There must be something else.

Here, based in part upon what we have learned till now, is my suggestion.

We begin by thinking about the famous Rashbam at Shemos 13:9. The *pasuk* reads: It shall be for you a sign on your arm and a reminder between your eyes—so that HaShem's Torah may be in your mouth—for with a strong hand HaShem removed you from Egypt.

Rashbam comments:

Careful reading demands that the phrase be understood to mean, "It shall serve as a cue upon your arm," meaning that it shall be a reminder to you *as though it were written upon your arm.* This would parallel the phrase in Shir HaShirim 8:6, *Consider me to be as though I were a medallion that you carry over your heart.*

Similarly between your eyes means, *as though it were an ornament that people are accustomed to wear between their eyes.*

Predictably, this radical interpretation called forth a forceful repudiation, in this case by Ibn Ezra.

I will offer a paraphrase of Ibn Ezra's objections and then examine it closely to see how we can make use of it for our problem. In essence what I will attempt to do is to find a compromise between Rashbam and Ibn Ezra.

Here then is the paraphrase:

Rashbam's contention had been that, at the *peshat* level,* it is possible to understand the two verses metaphori-

---

* Needless to say, Rashbam put on tefillin every morning. He did not deny that there was such a mitzvah. His contention was only that the source of this mitzvah was in the Oral Law rather than in the Torah text, which demanded to be understood metaphorically.

cally. When the Torah tells us that the truths that were just taught were to be placed upon our arms as a *cue*, no physical action need be contemplated. The meaning is simply that we ought to have these ideas constantly in our thoughts—as are objects that are actually tied to our arms. As precedent for such a use of language he cites references from Mishlei (really from Shir HaShirim, but there are similar usages in Mishlei).

Ibn Ezra is horrified. How can anybody claim that the Torah speaks metaphorically? *Mishlei* is different because it introduces itself as a book of parables (*Mishlei Shlomo ben David*), and therefore the use of metaphors is expected and acceptable. But if we were to countenance the use of metaphors in the Torah, that could turn everything on its head.

However, even Ibn Ezra admits that a category exists in the Torah where we willy-nilly need to interpret metaphorically. That is when the literal meaning would simply make no sense. *And you shall circumcise the blocks upon your hearts* cannot be rendered literally because there is no way that an actual heart could be circumcised. However, since in our *parshah* no such problem exists, there is no reason to read it in anything but the literal sense.

The phrase that Ibn Ezra uses, *We will therefore not explain it other than through the literal meaning,* is, so we would suppose, going to make life hard for Ibn Ezra. It works fine for tefillin. There is indeed nothing that forces us to assume that the Torah did not intend its words to be taken literally. None of us finds anything outlandish in putting on our tefillin in the morning. However, how does this work for *mezuzos* where a literal reading *is barred by the halachah.* The fact is that we do not, indeed may not, write *on* the doorposts.

But Ibn Ezra a few lines later is adamant that the phrase *and you shall write them on the doorposts of your house* is also to be taken literally. He refuses to countenance any other option. But how are we to understand this? Does the *halachah* that the mezuzah consists of a piece of parchment not stand in the way? The fact is that we *cannot* write the message *on* the doorpost?!

I think that the Netziv in *Ha'amek Davar* can help. Regarding the *pasuk You shall write them on your doorposts,* he explains that *"on"* is to be understood as fixing them onto the external doorpost with a nail. He seems to be saying much the same as the Ibn Ezra we have just quoted. But what does that mean? The words do not seem to yield the Netziv's interpretation, so in what sense do they "mean" that.

Here are a few thoughts on language in general. I am in no way an expert in the subject so please do not expect perfection. Still I feel that what I am about to write is not far from the truth. I will bring examples from English. I permit myself to do this, not because I am not aware of the fact that *lashon hakodesh* is different from other languages, but because relative to the *development* of language, a matter of people's psychological mind-set, I would assume at least a possibility of a certain degree of congruence.

In the first place it seems obvious to me that in any language a time comes when a metaphorical expression ceases to be a metaphor,* but slips into the regular language as a new meaning to a given word. When a principal tells an errant student that it is "with a heavy heart" that he is expelling him from school, he does not assume that the youngster will go through the process of "transfer" and figure out how and why "sorrow" is connected to "weight."** He just knows what a "heavy heart" is, and that is the most that you can expect from any language. Another example that we could easily "picture"*** would be an impatient parent who might tell a child who has come home with a once too often F that he or she is "tired" of hearing excuses.

* The word derives from Latin and Greek words meaning a "transfer."
** Actually there is a very close relationship. The ancestors of the word "sad" used to be synonyms for "heavy." A seventeenth-century dictionary describes a certain cheese as being "heavy and sad." (C. S. Lewis, *Studies in Words*).
*** I assume that you have caught my little trick here. Clearly this is another example.

Now, what about writing "on" something? Would we be pedantic and insist that these words can only mean what they say, or is there room for some flexibility? Would we be satisfied with having the message written on a piece of paper and sticking it where the writing was to have gone, something that, in practice, would have the same result? It seems to me that we come close to having an almost perfect example in English. The school is planning a Chanukah party and the principal suggests to the organizer, "Why not put an announcement on the bulletin board!" Now "to announce" derives from a Latin word meaning to "communicate by way of speech," "to deliver a message," and so on.* Now the principal does not mean that a tape machine should be affixed to the bulletin board in order to have the "announcement" made verbally. Paper will do fine.**

Accordingly I assume that this is what Ibn Ezra and the Netziv mean. Since the Torah uses the expression that it uses, and since we know that the *halachah* insists that parchment be used, we must assume that the expression *You shall write on* had already taken on the meaning that Netziv spells out. Everybody would have understood what the words mean.

Still, it seems to me that not all is well. At least in the first *parshah* of *kri'as Shema*, the mitzvah of mezuzah follows hard upon the mitzvah of tefillin. Why not use the same system for both? When it speaks of tefillin, the Torah mentions nothing about any boxes in which the message is to be contained. The text assumes that we are familiar with those from *Torah she'be'al peh*, the Oral Torah. So why not use the same formula with the mezuzah? Why not simply write something along the lines, *And fix them onto the doorposts of your houses,* assuming that we know the appropriate procedure through our tradition?

Then there is another problem. If one way or another the

* Trust me, I checked.
** The blurring of the differences between writing and some other form of communication can also be found in English. We can think of a boss telling his secretary, "Please take very careful note of the following. I want you to attend the meeting and to take notes!"

expression of writing had developed such that it was no longer required that the writing take place on the designated surface, but that it would suffice to have it done on a different object that could then be attached, then would we not have expected that this usage would occur in other places, too? I have done serious searches on the entire text of TaNaCh and have not been able to find any other place where this meaning was used.

We are ready to get back to our problem with the Rambam. We could not understand why, in the *Sefer HaMitzvos*, he would use *to make the* mezuzah. I will offer what I consider to be a possible explanation, which I will work out in the context of the disagreement between the Rashbam and the Ibn Ezra concerning the use of metaphors in the Torah.

I would like to suggest that even if we were to accept Ibn Ezra's argument that where the literal meaning makes sense it would be unacceptable to interpret a word or phrase metaphorically, *And you shall write on the doorposts of your house* would fall into the same category as *And you shall circumcise the blocks of your hearts*, which simply has no literal meaning. The fact that the *halachah* forbids writing the mezuzah text "on" the doorposts makes it necessary to find a meaning that is not communicated by a literal translation of the words.

However, according to the linguistic observations that we made earlier in this chapter, that expressions that started their literary careers as metaphors frequently end up as perfectly respectable, albeit new, dictionary meanings, we can claim that the same occurs here. "Family" members that authenticate the usage would be *write on your hearts* (Mishlei 3:3 and 31) and *shall write it upon their hearts* (Yirmiyahu 31:32). Just as in those phrases the meaning of "*kasav*" would not be to write, but to imbue the heart with a desired spirit, so, too, would our phrase command us (in a linguistically legitimate manner) to imbue our doorposts—guardians of the ambience that we wish to foster in our homes (see the ideas of Rav Hirsch quoted above)—with the values of the acceptance of the yoke of HaShem and his *mitzvos*.

Here, once more, is a paragraph that I wrote earlier in this chapter.

Have we come any nearer than we were earlier to a solution of the seemingly strange expression that the Torah uses when it tells us to *write these things* on the doorposts? It does not seem so. Although we have discovered—and a great discovery it is—that once the mezuzah has been affixed it becomes an integral part of the doorpost, does that mean that when I am *writing* the mezuzah it is upon the doorpost that I am doing so? The idea does not sit well with me. So why would the Ribono shel Olam write His Torah in a way that requires a leap of faith to understand it?

Although I originally wrote this paragraph just a few short days ago, much has happened in the meantime. We have all become aware of the possibility that the *kasav* family need not at all be limited to actual writing. It is a matter of imbuing the doorposts—and by way of the doorposts, the entire house—with a spirit that is energized by an acceptance of the yoke of heaven and the yoke of the *mitzvos*. We spoke earlier of the mezuzah burrowing into the woodwork of the doorpost and blending into it, and that, in fact, is a precise definition of its role. We are not informed of this by a creative use of metaphor, but that is the literal and only (*peshat*) meaning of the words that the Torah uses.

I wonder how many of you readers will agree with this, my final paragraph in this long chapter. If there is anything "creative" going on here, it is (perhaps) my suggestion for interpreting the Rambam's use of *making (asah)*. I wish to suggest that when Rambam in the *Sefer HaMitzvos* writes *to make the* mezuzah, he means "to turn a piece of parchment *into a doorpost*." If this sounds too much like *derush*, I apologize. It is the best that I can do with a, at least for me, really difficult issue.

15.

Mezuzos and Tefillin

*A*fter the long and complicated chapter that we have just completed, I feel that if we were asked what the purpose of the mezuzah on our doorposts might be, we could answer quite confidently.

We have not yet done much about tefillin, so we want to spend this chapter trying to figure out how to answer the same question about them. Let us spell it out this way. As we learned in the previous chapter and shall continue to discuss as we go along, the language of the Torah makes very clear that the mezuzah relates to the house in a way that is radically different from the way the tefillin relate to the person who wears them. The mezuzah defines the *home*; it turns it into an incubator that lays the groundwork for a successful encounter with the outside world. The tefillin *adorns* the *wearer*; it makes him into the ambassador of the Ribono shel Olam to a largely uncomprehending and often uninterested world.*

The mezuzah, as it were, burrows into the woodwork of the doorpost and blends into it; hence its change of name. From being a simple piece of parchment it turns into a mezuzah, a doorpost. As we learned from Rav Samson Raphael Hirsch in the previous chapter, it defines the house, turning it into an incubator where, nurtured by its messages, we become prepared for a fully Jewish life.

---

* See Shabbos 57a and b. The Mishnah on 57a lists *totafos* among the ornaments that women wear and 57b describes it as one that is worn on the forehead. Ramban, in his Chumash commentary (Shemos 13:16), argues forcefully that it is this ornamental aspect that the Torah has in mind when it refers to the *tefillin shel rosh* as *totafos*. He writes: *The Sages were, after all, native speakers for whom Hebrew was the natural language and therefore they knew precisely how this word was used. They are the true arbiters for the correct usage of that word.*

The tefillin do not define the person who wears them any more than any piece of jewelry that we put on would define us. People wear jewelry to impress, to charm, to distract, or for many other similar, often unedifying reasons. The tefillin, too, send a message,* but it is one that is vital and holy. "These are the values that I espouse; these are the ideas that matter to me. And so should they to you!"

Why?

Let us spend a couple of minutes thinking about Berachos 6a, the source that we quoted in the first footnote below. Why is it that the nations of the land will tremble in the presence of an *ehrlicher Yid* adorned by his *tefillin shel rosh*?[1]

We could give an answer that is short and to the point. I am going to take a little longer than is strictly necessary, so that we can get where we need to get. The issues involved are just too important for a more cursory treatment. Come along on this exploratory trip. You are not risking much and, in the end, I think that you will be happy that you did not make a fuss.

Quite frequently, the Rambam ends a series of *hala-chos* with a short hortatory** passage. In *Hilchos Tefillin, UMezuzah VeSefer Torah* he offers two of those: one at 4:25 upon completion of the section dealing with tefillin, the other at 6:13 rounding off the *halachos* of mezuzah.

I think that much can be gained by presenting these two next to each other.

---

* See Berachos 6a: *And all of the nations of the land shall see that the Name of HaShem is upon you and they will fear you (Devarim 28:10)...these are the tefillin shel rosh.*

** Here is a dictionary definition of "hortatory": Urging or exciting to some course of action, with strong arguments, appeals or advice.

MEZUZAH, 6:13	TEFILLIN, 4:25
All of us are obliged to take the mitzvah of mezuzah very seriously...since when a mezuzah is affixed to our doors, we will, every time we either come home or leave, come face-to-face with God's singularity.	The sanctity of the tefillin is great indeed. As long as they are tied to our heads and arms we will surely be both modest and God-fearing. We will not at all be attracted by any levity or useless patter. Certainly we will not permit our minds to engage in inappropriate thoughts.
We will remember our obligation to love the Ribono shel Olam and will wake up from the follies and stupidities that throughout our lives would otherwise be our constant companions.	Our minds will be fully engaged with matters concerning truth and righteousness.
Our minds will be thoroughly straightened out and we will realize that in this world nothing really matters at all except our knowledge of the Rock of the Ages.	Ideally we will be wearing the tefillin all day. That is what this mitzvah really demands.
Our Sages taught us that whoever is wearing tefillin on his head and arm, tzitzis on his clothes, and has a mezuzah affixed to his doorpost can be assured that he will likely not sin. He has four alert angels watching over him.	It was said of the great Rav who was a student of the holy R. Yehudah HaNasi that throughout his life nobody ever observed him walking even just four cubits without being engaged in Torah thoughts, and without wearing tallis and tefillin.

We begin with the opening phrase:

All of us are obliged to take the mitzvah of mezuzah very seriously...since when a mezuzah is affixed to our doors, we will, every time we either come home or leave, come face-to-face with God's singularity.	The sanctity of the tefillin is great indeed. As long as they are tied to our heads and arms we will surely be both modest and God-fearing.

It seems very clear to me that there is a sharp contrast between these two. In the tefillin section the Rambam's concern is the sanctity that overtakes the person who wears them. Rambam seems mesmerized by the sheer wonder of *holy living*. In the mezuzah section he is concerned with the mitzvah. Care must be taken to follow directions punctiliously.

This difference can be traced and recognized throughout the two passages. Let us see what happens when we wear our tefillin and have affixed our *mezuzos* to our doors. In the tefillin passage, Rambam uses...*we will surely* BE *both modest and God-fearing*. In the mezuzah passage we are told that...*we will* COME *face-to-face* with God's singularity. The tefillin passage speaks of *being;** the mezuzah passage speaks of *doing.***

In this context I find the following language of the Rambam particularly moving. *We will not at all be attracted by any levity or useless patter.*

Perhaps I am making too much of this; nevertheless, I will share my thoughts with you. In the light of the following Rambam passage I feel that the choice of the phrase...*will not be attracted* takes on great significance. Here is a passage from *Hilchos Dei'os* 6:1.

It is part of human nature to be attracted in his attitudes and behavior by the standards of his friends and neighbors and, in general, to act according to the norms of his fellow citizens.

Because of this it is essential that we should be friendly with righteous people and to live near the wise so that we should learn from them, but to keep far away from the wicked because we would be liable to be attracted by their ways.

Do you see what I am getting at? In *Hilchos Dei'os* the Rambam goes out of his way to stress that our tendency to

---

* The tefillin "are" on his head. We are passive. We "are" humble people and so on.

** We enter and exit. He is active. We "encounter" *yichud* and so on.

feel attracted to our surroundings is a psychological fact of life. It is simply the way we are. Nevertheless, with tefillin on our heads, when the Name of HaShem is called upon us, that entirely natural tendency simply evaporates. From being attracted, we are no longer attracted.

If you remember, we were drawn into this analysis when we wondered why the nations of the land would be terrified when they would see a *Yid* wearing his tefillin *shel rosh*. The ethereal beauty, the "real article," the true truth, is scary to those of us who are mired in the most pernicious of all lies. They whisper to us (or roar at us) of wasted potentials, of ugly indulgences, of stupefying folly.

There are no words that are sadder than the truly devastating "might have been."

We have one more chapter to go and then we will be done. However, before we get there, the following needs to be said. If you recognize yourself and your daily *Shacharis davening* in these descriptions of what tefillin are supposed to do to us, how fortunate are you! If, as I suspect, many of you, many of *us*, do not, then we have some serious work ahead of us.

Here is an exercise that you might enjoy—but then again you might not. Try saying the "tefillin" Rambam that we have now been considering, in the first person. Here goes:

> When I am wearing my tefillin *shel rosh*, I become modest and God-fearing. Laughter and senseless conversation no longer attract me and inappropriate thoughts never even cross my mind. There is no room in my heart for anything other than truth and righteousness.

If this does not seem to describe anybody you know intimately, you should be drawing some conclusions! Let me make a suggestion. Please check out the following endnote.[2]

16.

Let Us Learn to Live in the Mezuzah's Embrace

We have reached the final chapter of this book. We have covered a lot of ground. If each one of us were really to absorb every one of the suggestions that we have made, a lot of good things would happen to the way we practice our Judaism. But, and here is the bad news, that is not likely to happen. It is just very, very hard to change a lifetime of arid thoughtlessness into serious and responsible commitment. Growing up is hard to do. I know this from my own experience. Nevertheless, some little things *did* stick with me and I am optimistic that over time there will be more. Perhaps your experience will parallel mine.

I cannot explain the process that makes just those selections that left their mark for me work better than the others. I suppose that particular souls resonate to particular religious stimuli. But *how* it works is less important than *that* it works.

Although I did not particularly plan it this way, it is meaningful to me that I am bringing this book to an end with a contemplation of the mezuzah. It is really the mezuzah that started me on the path that eventually led to this book. Somehow, I had come across the passage in the Rambam (*Sefer Torah* 6:13) that I quoted fully in the previous chapter, and it hit me painfully how totally removed I was from the ideals that he expresses. Never, ever had going into or out of a door done anything for me religiously. As far as I was concerned, the mezuzah was something you stuck on the doorpost and forgot.*

* I know that many people kiss the mezuzah in passing—I personally had not been taught as a child to do that, so I never got into the habit—but I assume that they do so in gratitude for the protection that it offers (see Mezuzah 1). Anecdotal evidence that I gathered seems to confirm this.

I asked many friends about their experiences with the mezuzah. A hundred percent of them smiled sheepishly and admitted that this particular Rambam did not impinge on their lives in any practical way.

I drew what I believe to be the requisite conclusion from this sorry state of affairs, and the book that you are now reading is the result.

So let us get back to the mezuzah.

* * *

By this time I think that we have all absorbed the concept that, somehow, the mezuzah defines what we would like to be the spirit that permeates the house or, perhaps better, the home, to which it is attached. It is time to think about what position the family home plays in the hierarchy of values that the Torah espouses.

If you have access to the Yalkut Shimoni (Bemidbar, *Remez* 773), please check it out. It points to the fact that the censuses executed in the wilderness were interested not only in the tribes, but also in the families that were the building blocks from which the tribal units were constructed. Israel, in contrast to the pagan nations who knew nothing of marital morality, could produce their genealogical records, which testified to the absolute integrity of each family. It was that astounding purity that persuaded the Ribono shel Olam that the Jewish people were worthy recipients of the Torah.

Indeed it appears that the Jewish family stands close to the very center of our defining glory. We cannot do better than to ponder the following excerpts from the Hirsch commentary to Shemos where he discusses the requirement that the Pesach Offering that was brought in Egypt be eaten specifically within the family circle.

Here are a couple of random paragraphs:

The individual home is not meant to be an isolated unit responsible only for itself. Rather each home is to serve as an incubator in which the nation's collective spirit is to be nurtured, and its mission carried out. Hence only one who is part of the Jewish nation may be a party of a

Jewish household. However, the collective national mission is so great and variegated that every home should develop its own unique segment of this mission, in its own way and in accordance with its own special qualities, richly diverse in respect to character tendencies and ability and position. Thus the nation's mission will be accomplished in its entirety through the concerted effort of all the individual units toward one common goal.

...

Just as the spiritual upbuilding of the Jewish people was based on separation into homes...so later on at the actual upbuilding of the nation, the foremost foundation in the counting of Israel was the family (*leMishpechosam*). The pride of Israel and the source of its immortality are its family life, governed by purity and modesty.

There is more, much more, all of it extremely interesting, but for our purposes these few sentences must suffice.

Once we understand that the family unit, really the *home* with all the delightful tremors that that simple word awakens within us, constitutes the building block of our peoplehood, we are in reach of a more mature understanding of the nature and function of the mezuzah. By being made up of less—only two *parshios* instead of the four contained in the tefillin—it is really made up of more! The two *parshios* that make up its content, the acceptance of the yoke of HaShem and the acceptance of His *mitzvos*, are the rock-bottom foundation upon which all else is built. With Hillel we can say *All else is commentary, go and learn*! By burrowing into our doorposts, by in fact actually "becoming" our doorposts, as implied by its name, it establishes the unit wherein the soul of all else rules supreme.

I think that we are now ready to think about the first *parshah* of *kri'as Shema*, where our precious mezuzah makes its first appearance, and where it clearly feels fully at home. Since we have to bid each other farewell at some point, there is probably no better place than *kri'as Shema* for breaking up and moving off, each in his/her unique direction. The time has come to put into practice some of what we have learned throughout this book.

* * *

We all know *kri'as Shema* pretty well by heart, so none of the phrases that we will ponder will sound strange to us. However, when we start thinking about cohesion and direction, those same phrases will become a little puzzling. Try this little test on yourself. How would you answer this question: What is the unifying theme of the passage? Why did just the particular *mitzvos* that are mentioned, and none other, make the cut? It is not so easy, is it?

Specifically, what are *"these things"* that are to find their place (*vehayu*) *"on your heart"*? The text does not really specify and Rashi, the always reliable guide through the complexities of Chumash, somehow does not appear to be consistent. Then there is the rather rare expression, AL *levavecha,* ON *your heart.* What does it mean and what does it demand of us?

Accusing Rashi of an apparent lack of consistency is a serious matter. Can I back up my claim? Well, let us put that to the test. Here, once more, is the question. What is covered by the expression *these things*? Is it local or is it global? Is it just the *parshah* of *Shema* or does it cover the Torah as a whole?

Before we look at the following chart, let us just spend a moment pondering the beauty of that grammatical drudge, the unassuming pronoun. It is a useful linguistic tool standing in, mostly for a previously mentioned noun, thereby avoiding grinding repetition. In our *parshah,* the attribution *them* in *And you shall teach* THEM *to your children; And you shall tie* THEM *as a sign; And you shall write* THEM are all pronouns standing in for *these things.* Now, the latter two, speaking as they do of tefillin and mezuzah, are obviously limited to the local verses. What about *And you shall teach* THEM *to your children* and the various expressions that follow hard upon it?

Please check out this chart, which traces Rashi's treatment of the various expressions.

SUBJECT	RASHI	TEXT
Obviously Torah as a whole	"That the words of Torah should be sharp in your mouth; so that if a person asks you a matter of Torah, you should not have to hesitate about it, but rather, say it immediately."	ושננתם (*veshinantom*) "You shall teach them."
Obviously Torah as a whole	These are your students.	לבניך (*levanechah*) To your sons
Obviously Torah as a whole	The main thing you speak of shall be nothing but them. Make them the primary thing and do not make them secondary.	ודברת בם (*vedibarta bam*) You shall speak of them.
Clearly, *kri'as Shema*	One might think that [one might have to recite *kri'as Shema*] even if he lay down at midday...In fact, it refers to the time of lying down and the time of arising.	ובשכבך ובקומך (*uveshachbecha uvekumecha*) When you lie down and when you rise.
Clearly *k'rias Shema*	These are the tefillin on the arm and the tefillin on the head.	וקשרתם לאות...והיו לטטפות...וכתבתם... (*Ukeshartom le'os ...vehayu letotaphos ...uchesavtom...*) Bind then as a sign upon your arm and let them be an ornament between your eyes. And write them...

What do we do?

In a brilliant tour de force, Rav Samson Raphael Hirsch offers this masterpiece:

> For in truth the purpose of the whole Torah is to teach us how to fulfill the love of God *with all your heart, with all your soul, and with all your means*. The *toros*, teachings, which free the mind and heart from delusions and passion and instill in them truth and noble thoughts, reveal to us how to love God *with all our hearts*. *Chukim*, the statutes that limit and sanctify the development of our physical and sensual being within the bounds of morality drawn by God, teach us how to love God *with all our souls*. *Mishpatim* and *mitzvos*, the social ordinances and commandments, which establish our communal lives on the principle of justice and duty, teach us how to love God *with all our means*.
>
> *Eidos*, the testimony that represents to us these truths and tasks through symbolic acts, and *Avodah*, the symbolic offering that consecrates us to all this life service by which we are to seek God's nearness, engage every aspect of our whole being and so teach us how to love God *with all our hearts and all our soul and all our means*.

R Hirsch appears to be saying that *parshas* Shema can really stand for, does in fact embody, the entire Torah. All the five rows in the diagram that we have just examined are really dealing with the entire Torah. Three of them speak of it in its fully realized form, while the last two, though abbreviated, cover at least potentially the same ground. In his hands the problem that we raised has simply shriveled. *These things* refers to the entire Torah. But that "entire Torah" can either be fully articulated (the first three references) or compressed into its essence.[1]

I truly believe that Rav Hirsch's insight can serve as the key that is able to unlock some of the mysteries that have still remained unexplained even after all the thinking that we have done. Take the previous chapter. There we spent some very interesting time thinking about the tefillin *shel rosh* as a crown that marks us as royalty. I blame myself now for not having wondered why the four *parshios* that are contained in there—a small sampling at best—should confer any kind of king-ship upon us. I am, after all, acquainted, if unfortunately only distantly, with the Mishnah in Pirkei Avos that postulates forty-eight levels of hard, hard struggles, before we can lay claim to the crown of Torah. I should have asked and, sorry, so, dear reader, should you.*

If, as Rav Hirsch teaches us, the first two paragraphs of *Shema* are representative of the entire Torah, this problem can be retired. I feel lighter already.

Then there is the expression, ON *your hearts*. My intu-ition, and a number of examples that we will quote in a mo-ment, persuade me that things take place *in* the heart, not *on* it. There is a well-known Midrash that lists all the many emotions and faculties that are associated with the heart. As I write, I have in front of me the version from the first *perek* of Koheles Rabba. I see: *The heart hates [as it says,] "You shall not hate your brother* IN *your heart"; the heart covets [as it says,] "You shall not covet her beauty* IN *your heart"*; and so on. There are relatively few instances that use *al*, upon, and it is highly interesting how the Midrash treats those.

We are told: *The heart is "mishtadel,"* allows itself to be per-suaded (that is, *allows itself to be imposed upon*), [as it says,] "And he spoke UPON the heart of the girl." We all recognize Sh'chem speaking to Dinah. My dictionary defines the root word *sh-d-l* with פ ת ה (*p-t-h*), to win over. As an example it cites *Yoma* 35b: "Potiphar's wife *mishtadlo* with words." Thus the meaning of *the heart is mishtadel* is "the heart permits itself to be persuaded." A perfect fit!

We are particularly lucky that the *midrash* also quotes our *pasuk* in *kri'as Shema*. Here is the citation. *The heart accepts*

---

* If you did ask, you are off the hook. If not, welcome to the club of the "un-thinking." As we have stressed throughout this book, it is dedicated to the idea that too many of the Jewish gestures that, happily, fill our days and nights, are performed unthinkingly—by rote. The present example could be utilized as a convenient *mussar* thought to stimulate us to change for the better.

things [as it says,] "And these things...shall be on your heart." The heart allows itself to be guided.* Not everything is to be allowed into its hallowed space.

This is very exciting. I think that we have discovered the real meaning of the use of the preposition *al* when used with the heart. It indicates mastery over the heart. Whatever the noun that the preposition serves might be (in our case *These things*) is put "over" the heart, that is, it is put into a position from which it exercises control of what is to be contained "in" the heart.**

We are now ready to venture on in our attempt to understand the first *parshah* of *kri'as Shema* a little better. The tone is set by the first *pasuk, Shema Yisrael, HaShem Elokeinu, HaShem echad.* I am not going to attempt a translation; it is not really necessary for our immediate needs. I am hoping that you readers will not object if I simply take *echad* (one) as implying what we would express with the English, *uniquely all-encompassing.* There is nothing, nothing at all, in our lives or experiences that falls outside the purview of God's interest and involvement. I cannot guarantee that this covers every nuance of *yichud*, but it will do for us in the present context.

The next *pasuk* then adjures us to love this "all-encompassing" God, *with your entire heart, your entire soul, and with all of your means,* that is, with a *parallel* all-inclusivity. God has offered us the (relative) totality of His being, and demands no less than that we return the favor. The relationship must incorporate all relevant aspects of our personhood. Moreover, as we have now discussed, that apparently total involvement and commitment is to determine our hearts' agenda. ("These things shall be on [*al*] your heart.")

---

* Another example of the use of *al* is from I Shemuel 1:13, "Chanah was speaking *al libah*," where Radak writes that it really means *in her heart* but that it uses *al*, meaning "on," to teach us that she, apparently, *directed* her heart to express the feelings that were riling within her. Once more we have the equivalent of *taking guidance.*

** Here is a quote from the Hirsch commentary: על לב *(al lev), wherever applied, to words or their content, denotes not only that the words are kept in mind, but that the words have influence and power over the heart.*

That, however, is not enough. The *parshah* continues.

And you shall teach them to your children: The Ribono shel Olam is indeed a "jealous" God. In return for His single-minded involvement in our well-being He asks everything from us and concedes nothing. It is not enough that our entire personhood (heart, soul, means) be involved. To all of us there is a "fourth dimension," our future, the immortality to which we lay claim through our children. They, too, must be co-opted to our commitment.

And you shall speak of them when you sit in your house: If the meaning of this passage is simply to demand our total immersion in Torah study, it seems strange that it should be presented in the same *pasuk* as our obligation to teach our children. At the risk of being accused of presenting *d'rash* as *pshat*, I suggest that this part of the sentence is a direct continuation of the earlier part. It teaches us that the best way to assure a successful passing of the "baton" to the next generation is by becoming a role model par excellence. The children get a real head start if the father is an understanding *masmid.*[2]

We have attempted to find a coherent structure that can explain the various details that have found a legitimate place in this first *parshah* of *kri'as Shema.* Can we see it through to the end? Do tefillin and mezuzah blend readily into this particular neighborhood as we have defined it?

Obviously they must. Else they would not be there.

First we are going to deal with tefillin.

And you shall tie them...on your arm, and they shall be...between your eyes: Earlier in this chapter we found that there is a fourth dimension to our lives—the future that we build for ourselves through our children. The tefillin *shel rosh,* worn proudly in the open for everyone to see, expands this move outward, beyond our family, to embrace the entire community.

Let us think back to the Rambam that we cited in the last chapter: *Because of [what we have learned concerning the experience of wearing* tefillin, *the changes for the better in our very being that they bring about], we should strive earnestly to wear them the entire day. That, in fact, was the Torah's intention. Ideally we*

should be wearing our tefillin *constantly.* That practice has largely
fallen into disuse because the level of sanctity required for
such a life is simply beyond us in our extremely reduced state.*

Let us then try to picture Jewish living as, ideally, it should
be lived. Yankel, an up-and-coming business mogul, has finished *davening Shacharis* and has time for a cup of coffee and
a bite before rushing off for a day full of meetings. He briefly
removes his tefillin in order to take care of his physical needs,
but when done, he immediately puts them on again. Of course
he is wearing them as he drives to Manhattan. The radio has
long been banned from the car; listening would obviously be
incompatible with the *kedushah* in which he feels himself en-
veloped. He does not need its raucous silliness. Anyway, the
daf on his iPod takes up his time (though, as long as he is driving, not his absolute concentration) and, more important, his
interest.

He always enjoys his visits to his insurance guy. The palpable sanctity of the place gets to him. The principal in his
ornate office—wearing tefillin; the chief accountant, the ac-
tuary, the salesman with whom he deals—all wearing tefillin,
each in his own way contributes to an atmosphere in which no
whiff of chicanery could ever befoul the air. He particularly
likes the little luxuries that come with his financial standing.
He times his visit so that he will still be at the office when the
boot-black, a permanent fixture of the fancy office building,
makes his rounds—needless to say wearing tefillin.

You get the point. Our *tefillin shel rosh*, proudly displayed
and visible to everybody, creates an ambience of its very own,
way beyond the confines of the family circle.³ *Tefillin* have
certainly earned their place in this *parshah*. They have finally
rounded off the all-inclusivity that is demanded of us in reaction to the *echad* with which we are confronted by the Ribono
shel Olam.** ⁴

---

* I understand that there exist among us a tiny number of holy individuals
who maintain or at least try to approximate this ideal.

** You may find it useful to spend a little while with endnote 4. It could be argued that it deals with issues that really belong in the main body of the chapter, but I felt that it would just make things too complicated. Safely out of sight

Mezuzah

And you shall write them on the doorposts of your house: And what is left for the mezuzah to do? Have we not covered all the bases in this remarkable *parshah*? Well, at this point I can only say that the answer to this really very reasonable question resides somewhere or really everywhere in the four long and difficult chapters of which we are now writing the last sentences. The answer can really be stated very briefly. The mezuzah makes the cut because it is needed to facilitate all the vastly demanding efforts that lie implicit in the demands that the first *parshah* of *kri'as Shema* makes on us. It is there to help us become *ehrliche Yidden*.

ואידך פירושא

ALL ELSE IS COMMENTARY.

זיל גמור!

GO AND LEARN!

We have reached the end of this book. If you are still with me at this point, you will know exactly what I mean when I say that each of us could probably write another several books continuing the theme that we have been pursuing here. The sad truth is that, unless we are willing to go through life as "Jews, grade B," we all need a good shaking up. None of the matters that we took up in this book concern esoteric* issues that do not impinge upon our daily lives. Can you imagine how much more vital, more inspiring, more supportive of our theoretical beliefs and attitudes all those words that we speak and actions that we perform would be if we took the trouble to really think of what we are saying and doing?!

Enough said.

Now, let us spend a few moments on those several books that you all are planning to write. Let me start you off with a topic that you might want to explore. Since the last few chapters put us all in the mezuzah and tefillin mode, let us take our topic

---

with the endnotes, it will not be as threatening and, if you feel like it, you can view it at your leisure.

* Dictionary definition: Confined to and understandable by only an enlightened inner circle.

from that same area. We put on tefillin every day, but we* also take them off. Is that just a negative—we have finished with them for the day and no longer have the need to wear them— or are positive religious values involved? If you recall the end-note to chapter 1, where we learned what Rav Hirsch deduced from the fact that the final *kiddush yadayim veraglayim* that the *kohen gadol* performed on Yom Kippur was when he finally divested himself from his priestly garments and put on his regular clothing, my question here will not sound as outlandish as perhaps it did when you first read it.

If you take a look at Orech Chaim 25:13 and in the *Mishnah Berurah* (56) you will find that it is not at all simple to determine when, toward the end of davening, we ought to begin taking off our tefillin. For me, what I learned there came as a shock. If anybody would have asked me why we wear tefillin during our *Shacharis* davening, I would have suggested that they are required for *Shema* and *Shemoneh Esrei*. It would not at all have occurred to me to take the number of *kadeishim* and *kedushos* into account. And yet it seems that just these have a profound effect upon the usages that are being discussed in that section of the Shulchan Aruch.

As you begin thinking about why that might be so, you may recall my contention in chapter 1 that, in my opinion, the *berachah oter Yisrael besifarah* is the very peak of *Birkos HaShachar*. There, I promised that we would get to an explanation in its own good time. Well here, at the very end of the book, that time may have arrived for you. Is taking off the tefillin and changing that crown for our weekday hats not reminiscent of the *kohen gadol* taking off his priestly garments and changing into his regular clothing? And did we not learn...

There you have it. I can't wait to see chapter 1 of all those books that all of you will surely be writing—if not for publication, at least in your hearts.

May you be successful in your efforts.

---

* I offer my apologies to the ladies who might be reading this book. We are talking theory here and I am quite certain that you will not encounter any difficulty with the direction that I am suggesting for your research.

Notes

Introduction

1. Please see the footnote on page 2. Rav Hirsch's insistence that we understand the text as we have indicated is meant to avoid a major problem. The Gemara appears troubled by only *yir'ah*. But the passage mentions a number of other qualities that are demanded of us. If *yir'ah* alone is difficult to come by, then certainly *yir'ah* + love + serving God with all our might and so on will be hard to attain. Why does the questioner limit himself to only *yir'ah*?

   Rav Hirsch's rendering takes care of this problem. Our task is to discover *yir'ah*. The other qualities listed by our passage will all follow in their own good time from the premises that *yir'ah* will inculcate in us.

2. For the sake of transparency I note that what I have written here does not accord with what the Ramchal writes under *zerizus*, alacrity, in his Mesilas Yesharim. He appears to understand this Mechilta as an exhortation against laziness and procrastination. I notice that in Ofeq Institute's wonderful edition of the *Complete Mesilas Yesharim* (page 346), they translate the relevant phrase, *that a person should not* delay *performing a mitzvah*. It is interesting that in the Dialog Version (page 95) they render the relevant passage as, *when a mitzvah comes your way do not allow it to turn sour through delay*.

   As I indicated in the chapter, I like Wikipedia's *lighter and softer*.

Prologue

1. If we are to inject meaning into our bowing when we say *Modim*, it makes sense to know what we are saying. The root word *y-d-h* (י ד ה) has a number of different meanings, of course loosely related to each other. It can mean *praise* (להודות ולהלל), *admit* (מודה במקצת, ודוי), and *expressing gratitude* (קרבן תודה, הודאה על שעבר). All three share a feeling of dependence upon the person (or Person) who is the object of our *hoda'ah*.

   Now the *Modim* prayer uses the root word *y-d-h* twice: מודים אנחנו לך שאתה..., *Modim anachnu loch sheAtoh*...(using the preposition *sh*, ש, *that*) and...נודה לך ונספר תהלתיך על חיינו, *Nodeh lecha unsaper tehilosecha al*...(using the preposition על, *for*). The second usage clearly is an expression of thanks for favors received; we thank *for* something. But that will not work in the first phrase. We do not "thank" that...So מודים אנחנו לך ש... cannot mean *we thank you*. Rav Hutner (*Pachad Yitzchak* on Chanukah 2:6) argues that in that phrase י ד ה is used in the sense *to admit* (or, in context, I suppose *avow* would be better). Of course the language supports this meaning: *We avow that You are HaShem our*

God...and so on. Only after we have affirmed that we understand "Who" the Ribono shel Olam *is*, do we turn to Him with gratitude, *Nodeh Lecha al*.

Once all this is understood, our bowing at the opening phrase of the blessing becomes perfectly clear. As we pronounce our recognition of "Who" the Ribono shel Olam is, we bow down before Him as a physical expression of our total submission.

The *halachah* as recorded in Orech Chaim 113:4 requires that, when we bow down during the *Amidah*, we bend sufficiently low that the vertebrae of the spine so to speak "come apart." That is a pretty hefty bow. When I look around in shul it strikes me that hardly anybody does this. Most of us seem satisfied with a formal little genuflection that, in halachic terms, does not go nearly far enough.

It strikes me that for anybody who really wants to experience *Modim* as it ought to be experienced, it would be a good idea to do the bending as it should be done. My own experience is that the physical act, when done correctly, can help a lot toward a meaningful and respectable thoughtfulness.

Chapter 1

1. Here is a quote from the *Mishnah Berurah* 4:1:

    The Rashba explains the need for a formal hand-washing in the morning, as follows. Waking up in the morning is really a kind of rebirth (in accordance with Eichah 3:23), *Every morning anew, I become aware of the vastness of Your constancy*. Consequently it becomes incumbent upon us to affirm to the Ribono shel Olam that He has created us in order to contribute to His honor, to serve Him, and to bless His name.

    In recognition of all this our Sages ordained certain blessings that we are to pronounce every morning, and also that we should "sanctify" ourselves by using a vessel from which to perform certain ablutions just as a real *kohen* was obliged to do before he began his Temple service.

Please note that it is not simply a matter of washing our hands for the sake of cleanliness. If that were all there was to it, no vessel would be required. As it is, the water is to be poured upon our hands from a vessel as a reminder of the *kohanim* who, upon entry into the Temple courtyard, had to wash their hands and feet from the *kiyor* in preparation for their divine service.

Of course there appears to be a problem. *Avodah* is a formal halachic category that pertains to the service in the Beis HaMikdash. Here we are talking of ordinary people getting out of bed on an ordinary morning, about to begin an ordinary day and fill it with ordinary work. What possible connection can any of this have to the Temple service of the *kohanim*?

We can get some help from R. Samson Raphael Hirsch's Chumash commentary to VaYikra 16:4. He is discussing the immersions and ablutions that were a part of the Yom Kippur service performed by the *kohen gadol*, the chief of the *kohanim*.

> Thus five *immersions in a mikveh*, and ten *ablutions of hands and feet with the water supplied from the kiyor, a basin installed in the courtyard of the* Beis HaMikdash, mark the transition from one *act of service*, to another. And great significance is attached to the *last ablution of hands and feet*, which he performs at the end of the day, *when he removes the sacred garments and puts on ordinary clothing* (Yoma 32a). From this we learn that not only the *divestiture of holy garments that is undertaken with the purpose of putting on other holy garments requires the ablutions*, but also the *divesting of holy garments with the intention of putting on ordinary clothes, requires a formal ablution at precisely the same level as the others*; that is to say, even removing sacred garments for the sake of donning ordinary, everyday clothing—this, too, constitutes an *act of divine service*.
>
> This then is the idea that concludes the order of the service of this day: The meaning of all the symbolic procedures performed in the sanctuary is in the actual life *outside* the Sanctuary. For ordinary life actualizes the spirit that is drawn in Sanctuary life. Indeed *the meaning of the aspirations in the holy vestments is in the deeds performed in ordinary, everyday clothes.*

Something to think about, is it not?

Chapter 2

1. The word *mal'ach* that we use for angel also carries the meaning of *agent*, one who is charged, and therefore empowered, with executing legal processes for the person who deputized him. In contrast to a human messenger who, even while he accepted the role of agent still maintains his own identity, the angel has no independent existence outside his mission. He has no personality other than what is implied by "agent." There cannot be any "time off," because outside his "agent" function he has no existence.

2. Noteworthy, but not problematic. There are also other groups of *berachos* where we can observe the same system. As one example we can take *Birkas HaMazon* whose four *berachos* certainly form a coherent grouping (see further along in this book) and where nonetheless the first *berachah* is in the third person while the others are in the second.

   Needless to say, the fact that such a system is occasionally used does not free us from trying to understand why this should be so.

3. Please see the previous endnote. In switching persons within the same *berachah, Asher Yotzar* is also not unique. Think of the first *berachah* preceding *kri'as Shema* in the morning. Until the very end it is couched in the

third person. Then, beginning with the words *May you shine a new light...*it switches to the second. (Please note that not all *minhagim* have this text.)

4. I believe that this thesis explains the use of the unusual term *lifnei chisei chevodecha* (*before the throne of Your glory*). My search program yielded that mention of this throne is fairly frequent in the *nusach Sefard* of the siddur, but hardly at all in *nusach Ashkenaz*. So why use it here instead of the perfectly serviceable *lefanecha* (*before You*)? However, from the frequent appearance of the term *kisei* on Rosh Hashanah when there is much talk of the *kisei hadin* (*the throne of justice*) and the *kisei harachamim* (*the throne of mercy*), it seems clear that the *kisei* is the place from which the Ribono shel Olam exercises His providence over human affairs. Here it is not the God of Justice or Mercy that is being invoked, but the Healing God, to Whom we look to keep our bodily functions in healthy balance.

5. I heard a beautiful story from the late R. Noach Weinberg. An acquaintance who owned an old age home told him that he had once persuaded a ninety-year-old lady to become a *ba'alas teshuvah*. This was a story that R. Weinberg felt that he had to hear. He asked his friend how he could have brought off such a miracle.

   The home had only non-Jewish clients and was therefore able to serve non-kosher meals. One day a Jewish woman moved in. He explained to her that he would be unable to serve her the regular meals but that he would supply her with food that was much superior to that which everybody else received. She adamantly refused. She wanted to be like everybody else. When a government inspector came by to see that the home was run as it should be, she complained that the owner was discriminating against her. The inspector told the owner that unless he complied with the lady's request, the inspector would close down the facility.

   "And so," the man concluded, "I made her into a *ba'alas teshuvah*."

   Rabbi Weinberg protested. "But, you have not explained how you did it. It was that which piqued my interest."

   The man replied, "This way, that way, what is the difference! They were going to close me down. I had no alternative!"

   Rabbi Weinberg used this story to make the point that when people involved in *kiruv* sometimes fail, it is only because they consider failure to be a legitimate option. If failure would simply be unthinkable, they would find a way.

   For that kind of persuasiveness you need the intimacy of a face-to-face relationship. If the owner of the home had written the most eloquent essay, he would still have been closed down.

Chapter 5

1. In the meantime, more or less for the fun of it, let us consider how they felt about this issue in Kelm, the famous *mussar* yeshiva in Lithuania where, over a period of nineteen years, Rav Dessler became "Rav Dessler." Here is

an English paraphrase of a paragraph from the introduction to the first volume of the famous *Michtav MeiEliyahu*.

> Everything, but really everything, in Kelm centered upon education. R. Dessler used to reminisce how over a period of many years the lady relative at whose house he used to eat served him nothing at all but a dish made of oats that had absolutely no taste. She did this in order to train him to be undemanding in his physical needs. *Rebbi* used to smile when he told this story and made the point that the lady was completely successful in her efforts. After years of such an education, for the rest of his life there was no food that did not taste delicious to him.

2. For example, *Blessed is He who provided a delightful scent to fruits,* and similar *berachos*. The Gemara in Berachos 43b seems to take this all for granted. Said Rav Zutra bar Tuvia in the name of Rav Tuvia, Rav said: How do we know that we make a blessing on a fragrance? It says, "Every soul shall praise God." What gives pleasure to the soul and not the body? Only fragrance.

3. Here is an excerpt from my recent book, *For Rashi's Thoughtful Students* from the chapter entitled "Rashi's Choices."

> We are expected to realize that the *Kodesh HaKodoshim* is an extraterritorial area in our physical world that is not governed by the physical limitations that we normally take for granted. Here is a quote from Yoma 21a: Said Rabbi Levi, We have a tradition that the place on which the ark rested did not conform to the normal rules of space.

Here is the Rashi to this strange passage.

> The area that the ark occupied does not count. It does not take up space in the room. In spite of the fact that it was placed in the center of the room, the twenty-by-twenty-*amos* area in the room was in no way diminished.
>
> There are many other details that demonstrate conclusively that the laws of physics were simply suspended in the *Kodesh HaKodoshim*. It is as we have said. That entire area was extraterritorial. It hinted at a world that lies entirely outside our experience.

4. See Berachos 48b where we learn that the first three *berachos* were instituted, respectively, by Moshe Rabbeinu, Yehoshua, with the third one attributed partly to King David and partly to King Solomon.

> The fourth *berachah* was instituted after the Second Temple had already been destroyed. It was added to the *Birkas HaMazon* in order to commemorate the miracles that happened during the tragic years that followed the defeat at Beitar. During the siege the Romans had not permitted any egress from Yerushalayim, thus preventing the dead from being buried. When these unfortunates were ultimately brought to burial, it was found that none of them had decomposed. The fourth

berachah was added to celebrate these two wonders: that they were ultimately brought to a respectable burial and that the bodies had not become decomposed.

Chapter 6

1. Here is a small excerpt from my book *I Brought You Unto Me* on the *Aseres HaDibros*. It is on page 69 in the chapter entitled "The Fourth *Dibrah*." It will make you feel either good or bad. Personally, it makes me feel awful.

    The background is as follows. Many commentators are troubled by the phrase, *la'asos es haShabbos*. The word *la'asos*, of course is built from the root word ע שׂ ה (*ah-s-ah*), *to make*. The problem lies in the fact that in most of our minds Shabbos is a day of abstention (from work), not of creating or making. What do we "make" on Shabbos? As an example of how this problem is treated we might cite Ibn Ezra, who suggests that the word refers to Friday. "Make" Shabbos possible by taking care of all necessary preparations (traveling, cooking, and so on) in good time on Friday.

    Here is the quote from my book.

    > S'forno has a different approach and it is his idea that I would now like to consider. Here are his words: "The Bnei Yisrael are to keep Shabbos: in this world, in order to create (make) Shabbos: for the future, a Shabbos that will be eternal."

    > If I understand S'forno correctly, these few, seemingly simple words can literally change lives. He proposes nothing less than that, on Shabbos, we ourselves, each one for his or her self, creates [hence the active ע שׂ ה] their own Olam HaBa. As we keep Shabbos we are building a home for ourselves wherein we will spend eternity, a long, never-ending Shabbos.

    > What a thought!

    > Now, Seforno does not make the following point, but I suspect that it is what he had in mind. Berachos 57b teaches that Shabbos is *me'ein* Olam HaBa, that it embodies elements of Olam HaBa. Given that, it seems to me to make sense to reason that the way I spend my time on Shabbos, the degree to which I am awake to its whisperings, how I carry myself, the words I speak and the words I do not speak, all tell some very revealing stories concerning my suitability as a citizen of Olam HaBa. Shabbos is speaking to me, am I listening? Do I know how to appreciate its magnificent offerings or am I focused on my nap? Would an *"Olam-HaBa-dicker Yid"* want to spend Shabbos at my house or would he not? Would he feel that he had met a kindred spirit or would he look at me pityingly as an illiterate alien in the world of Shabbos?

    > We all have some thinking to do. No?

Chapter 7

1. I am avoiding the term mitzvah *kiyumis*, a technical term used in Gemara study that describes the credit that accrues to a woman who, although formally relieved of a given command that binds a man—let us say eating in a *succah*—nevertheless does so voluntarily. For her the mitzvah of *to dwell in a succah for seven days* is not a mitzvah *chiyuvis*, a binding mitzvah, but an act that may be considered meritorious (and qualifies as a mitzvah) if she chooses to fulfill it. Both terms refer to the same mitzvah that is recorded in the Torah. For the man it is a *chiyuv*, obligatory, for her it is a *kiyum*, an opportunity to garner merit by *fulfilling* it.

   That is not the case here. There is no claim that the mitzvah of *On the evening [of Pesach] you shall eat matzos* (Shemos 1:18) that binds us on the night of the fifteenth, remains voluntary throughout the Yom Tov. That is manifestly not the case. *On the evening* cannot in any sense be said to refer to anything other than the first evening of Pesach. Rather, eating matzah after the first night could be considered to be a (nonbinding) mitzvah in "fulfillment" of one of the other verses in the Torah that speak of eating matzah throughout the Yom Tov. An example of this would be the very verse that contains the binding mitzvah. The verse reads, *On the first, on the fourteenth day of the month, in the evening, you shall eat matzos, until the evening of the twenty-first day of the month.* The second part of the verse that deals with the rest of the Yom Tov does not rise to the level of a binding mitzvah, but hints at the fact that the Ribono shel Olam would consider it to be a meritorious deed.

   For further elucidation, please see the Chizkuni that I quote in the body of the chapter.

2. Interestingly enough, it makes the *whole* Pesach, not only the first night when the affinity for speed was actually manifest, into a celebration of the timelessness of the Divine impress. Please take the time to read our discussion of Devarim 16:2–3. You will not regret it

Chapter 9

1. I suspect that our obligation to make a *berachah* before indulging in most physical pleasures (Berachos 35a, אסור לו לאדם שיהנה מן העולם הזה בלא ברכה) derives from this situation. There is, after all, no such requirement from a non-Jew. We have no rights here and, consequently, must pay our dues. The non-Jews (loosely grouped under Eisav) are owners of record. They owe nothing to anybody.

2. Earlier in this chapter I raised two questions. Why was such a cumbersome sign required to identify the people who lived in the various homes; and why, of all things, blood? I have tried to deal with the first issue but left the second unexplored. It seemed to me that there would simply be too much of it and our treatment of Pesach would lose its focus. The literature must

be full of countless explanations and those of you readers who want to follow this up will not find it difficult to turn up any number of ideas. If you have access to the Shemos volume of the Hirsch Chumash, you might find it interesting to read up on this issue. Rav Hirsch understandably lavishes many, many pages of analysis on the Pesach Offering and, as always, entering into his thought world is an unmitigated delight. You will find a discussion of our problem on a couple of pages beginning on page 170.

Chapter 10

1. Hearten yourself and learn *siman* 529 in Orech Chaim. The title is *Dinei Simchas Yom Tov, The Laws That Tell Us How the Joys Associated with Yom Tov Are To Be Experienced.* Here is a quote from section 2: *We are called upon to rejoice on the festival: he, his wife, his children, and all those who are joining him in his celebration. How does he make everyone happy? He gives the children nuts and toasted grains; he buys his wife clothing and jewelry…he eats and drinks and is happy on the festival.…*It sounds as though I got things wrong, does it not? There does not seem anything particularly uplifting about these forms of rejoicing. How do roasted grains and nuts, clothing and jewelry, meat, and wine (Pesachim 109a) contribute to the kind of joy that is generated by the fact that HaShem has chosen us?

   And yet, the Ribono shel Olam appears to trust us. The Shulchan Aruch goes on: *Let him not get too involved with the food and [come to indulge in] laughter and light-headedness. Such behavior constitutes stupidity; not happiness.* The *Mishnah Berurah* (21) makes the point that people (*chasidim*) who make it their life's striving to be constantly aware that they are in the presence of the Ribono shel Olam will express the good feelings generated by the Yom Tov atmosphere, with praises sung to Him as the source of their happiness.

   Apparently we are expected to be able to convert the feeling of well-being generated by nice clothes and tasty meals into nothing other than pouring out our hearts in praise and adoration of the Ribono shel Olam.

2. Please note that there are a number of mysteries surrounding the use of *cheirus* in this context. I believe that by the time you get to the end of this chapter these will be solved. However, at this stage I think it important that you should be aware of them.

   Before anything else, it strikes me as strange that we should be using a word that never, even once, occurs in the Torah. Even assuming that the word is indeed to be translated as *freedom*, there are two perfectly good words (*chofshi* and *dror*) that *do* occur with that meaning (albeit not in connection with *yetzi'as Mitzrayim*) and, so it seems to me, might just as well have been substituted. Then there is *g-a-al*, which is used at Shemos 6:7 *Vega'alti eschem*, to describe part of the Ribono shel Olam's promise of how He would bring about our emancipation. So *zeman ge'ulaseinu* would seem most appropriate of all.

The use of *cheirus* is not limited to the phrase that we are now discussing. I can think of at least two other places in the siddur where it is used. *Tekah bashofar gadol l'cheirusenu* comes to mind, as does *Vayotze es amo Yisrael mitocham l'cheirus olam*. Why introduce this apparently foreign term? The expression "foreign" is particularly apt in the present context. *Cheirus* and its derivatives such as *ben chorin*, (think of the Haggadah, *hashata avdei, l'shana haba b'nei chorin*), are not even Hebrew; they are Aramaic. The Targum on Chumash uses them constantly to translate the Hebrew *chofshi* and *dror* and, as noted above, they simply do not occur in Chumash for that very reason. The Radak in his *Sefer HaShorashim* does not bring *cheirus* at all, although he has both ח ו ר (*ch-o-r*) and ח ר ר (*ch-r-r*) among the root words that he defines.

So why would the authors of our prayers use an Aramaic word when the available Hebrew seems to be perfectly adequate?

As we go along in this chapter we will reach the conclusion that translating *cheirus* as *freedom* really misses the mark.

3. Who are the "*Kohanim*" in this description? It seems clear that the term is to be understood in its broadest sense, that is that it is not limited to the actual *kohanim*, the descendants of Aaron HaKohen, but that it includes the entire Jewish people (see Yeshayahu 61:6, *And you will be called kohanei HaShem*) who since receiving the Torah had become the *priestly kingdom*. This definition is espoused by R. Samson Raphael Hirsch (see at Shemos 19:6 and at VaYikra 11:1) and reflects the contents of *sefer* VaYikra. These (till the middle of Shemini) comprise the laws that apply to the sacrificial Temple service (required now since Shemos ended with the completion of the Tabernacle to the point that it was ready to go into service) that are, of course, addressed mainly to the actual *kohanim*. From there onwards until BeChukosai, the main subjects that are covered deal with those *mitzvos* that might (in general terms) be seen as assuring the *sanctity* of the *priestly kingdom and holy nation*. These comprise permitted and forbidden food (Shemini); the laws of *tumah* and *taharah* (in Tazria and Metzora); Yom Kippur and forbidden marriages (Acharei Mos and Kedoshim) and finally the laws of *Shemitah* and *Yovel* (BeHar).

The latter half of BeChukosai is taken up by the *tochachah* (warnings of retribution), which, as Ramban at the beginning of BeHar explains, constitutes the enactment of the covenant on the second set of *luchos*.

What then is the function of the first part of BeChukosai, the part that predicts what will happen if we follow the statutes of HaShem?

I believe firmly that it constitutes the grand finale to the *sugia of yetzi'as Mitzrayim*. Everything, but really *everything*, is now in place. We had left Egypt up to, and including, the predicted endpoint of *You will serve God on this mountain* (Shemos 3:12). We received the Torah (albeit in the *plan B mode* of the second *luchos*) and allowed ourselves to be constituted as a *kingdom of priests and a holy nation*. The first concern once that status had been reached was to make it possible for God's Presence to dwell among us and that was accomplished by the building and the ultimate inauguration of the Tabernacle, a process that is described in the *parshios* between Terumah and the first part of Shemini. However, the nation that is going to play host to the Divine Presence must live lives of sanctity not only while they are engaged in religious services but also in their daily lives. Therefore, immediately after the inauguration of the Tabernacle it became necessary to acquaint them with the laws that would lend holiness to their daily living. These govern the foods that they eat (Shemini), the conditions under which they are exposed to uncleanliness and the means by which they can rid themselves of such negative experiences (Tazria, Metzora), and the marriages that they are permitted to contract (Acharei Mos, Kedoshim).

The constant struggle to lead a holy life while living as aliens in a physical world that is full of insidious attractions needs periodic reinforcement. The Jewish year is punctuated by a series of holy days that, each in its own way, brings us face-to-face with the privileges and duties that devolve upon us from within the uniqueness of our history (Emor). These reminders are buttressed by the seven-year cycle of the *shemitah* years that at the end of fifty years culminate in the *Yovel*, the greatest degree of sanctity of them all (BeHar).

With that, *yetzi'as Mitzrayim* has really come to an end and we are ready for the rebuke in the second part of BeChukosai which constitutes the enactment of the covenant that binds us to the *kabbalas haTorah* of the second *Luchos*. (See *Ramban* at the beginning of BeHar.)

Where does that leave the first part of BeChukosai, the part that begins with the opening words, *if you will follow my statutes*?

You are ready to go back to the body of the chapter. Good luck!

4. The following could well, and perhaps should, have been dealt with in the chapter proper. I have decided to make it into an endnote in order to keep this difficult chapter as simple as possible.

Even at this early stage of our argument it seems clear that the demands made by section 1 would stand in absolute contrast to the accusations leveled against us in the *tochachah* section of BeChukosai. There the ubiquitous villain is running our lives with a *"keri"* attitude. If we can find an accurate translation for that slippery term, it should go a long way towards understanding section 1 accurately. The late R. Aryeh Kaplan provides a long list of possibilities on page 372 of *The Living Torah*. ArtScroll uses *casually, The Living Torah: to be indifferent*. Radak in *Sefer HaShorashim* suggests, *"You will say that the suffering that I bring upon you just happened to happen and is not to be considered as a punishment for your sins."* If I understand him correctly he seems to attach the same meaning to *mikreh lailah* (Devarim 23:11). He would render it, *a "happening" of the night.*

I think it best to accept Radak for the purpose of this chapter. Accordingly we shall try to show that section 1 expects such attitudes and behavior as is absolutely inconsistent with a *keri* philosophy. It demands that we live a life in which we realize with absolute clarity that even in this physical world we live always and constantly in the Ribono shel Olam's embrace. Nothing, but nothing, just happens. (This final sentence is based upon Ramban to Shemos 13:16 [toward the end]. There is much to be said on this issue—see Ramban to Bereishis 18:19—but in the present context there is no need to examine it in detail.)

Please now return to the chapter.

5. As long as we have quoted from the *Igros Chazon Ish* in the chapter proper, it seems appropriate to quote from letter 20 in which he laid down appropriate usages for a yeshiva *bachur* who had apparently asked his advice. There are altogether six behaviors that the Chazon Ish recommends. Of these, the first and longest reads as follows:

> By all possible means you should avoid eating simply for the pleasure that it gives you. Just as our bodies are subject to impurities, so are our precious souls. Do not sully your soul. The practice of self-indulgence drags us down to the furthest depths. It most certainly gets in the way of productive Torah learning. Chazal taught that rather than pray that Torah might "enter" into our lives, we should pray that delicious food not enter our bodies. They advised us to withdraw our hands from any meal that promises us delicious tastes.

6. In the imagery of the Torah, servitude is pictured as a yoke. Thus we have (Bereishis 27:40), *And you will serve your brother, [but] when you will have cause to complain about his ascendancy (because he does not live up to his obligations—see Rashi), you will remove his yoke from your neck.*

It is worth noting in passing that care must be taken in choosing appropriate metaphors. Different cultures may look upon a given object from different perspectives and a metaphor that is enlightening and hits the mark in one language may be unable to do the job in a different one. The "yoke" is a good example. Dictionaries trace the word to early forms that have the meaning of joining two things together, of uniting things. This came about because generally oxen work in teams of two. Thus the English "yoke," at least in its original incarnations, would not serve well as a metaphor for slavery. However, in *lashon hakodesh* there are very many references to the heavy weight of the yoke and the oppressive burden that it imposes. As a metaphor it is a perfect fit.

To understand the imagery in this *pasuk* I would suggest that you get hold of the ArtScroll Chumash with Rashi, which has a useful diagram to show the respective functions of the actual yoke and the pegs that hold together the reins joined to the yoke. I found it very useful. The Ribono shel Olam promises to smash those pegs; the whole yoke will come undone and, released from its weight, we will be able to resume our ideal upright posture.

As I was thinking about our *pasuk* together with the Bereishis one that I cited earlier, it struck me that the difference in wording would certainly not be coincidental. In our *pasuk* the imagery is of the yoke as a foreign object that does not really belong on the proud ox but is imposed upon it by the baleful pegs that do not permit it to be removed. Break those pegs and the yoke can simply be shrugged off. The Eisav model is different. Yaakov, by dint of the *berachos* that were rightfully his, has the right to impose the yoke upon Eisav; it is where it is supposed to be. It is only when Yaakov abuses that right (*When you have cause to complain*) that Eisav, by brute force, is able to reject his servile position.

7. At this time we should take care of a technical issue that, while it does not impact directly on the thesis that we are building up in this chapter, should still be considered within the context of our discussion.

   Kidushin 31a (codified in Orech Chaim 2:6) rules that it is forbidden to walk four cubits in an erect posture and that whoever does so is *pushing aside the Divine Presence*. While it is difficult to pin down precisely what is meant by this latter phrase, it certainly indicates a degree of unseemly pride. Me'iri equates it with arrogance (*azus metzach*).

   If an *erect posture* is so bad, why is it so good?

   In a rather cursory search I have not been able to find anyone who asks this question. I feel comfortable with the following suggestion, although I cannot, of course, vouch for its truth. I suggest that there is such a thing as an inner *erect posture* that is, not connected with physical posture. It is a matter of how one perceives oneself. It is more a matter of healthy self-confidence than of straight shoulders. Certainly one would suppose that in leaving Egypt surrounded by the Clouds of Glory, that is in the almost tangible presence of the Ribono shel Olam, nobody would have felt like walking around with a swagger. It is the outer manifestation, not the inner attitude, that is condemned in the Kidushin passage.

8. There is a beautiful story concerning the late, great Rav Moshe Feinstein who was the rosh hayeshiva of Yeshivas Tiferes Yerushalayim. A major donor, who, as is usual with major donors, was in a major rush, was cooling his heels in the office waiting, while the rosh hayeshiva was *davening Minchah* in the *beis hamidrash*. Apparently much was at stake, and the yeshiva's director was getting more and more panicked as the minutes ticked by.

   Unable to contain himself, he rushed to the *beis hamidrash* to hurry the rosh hayeshiva back to his meeting. He saw that the rosh hayeshiva had, in fact, already finished his *tefillah* but was "unable" to take the required three steps backward because a youngster stood behind him, still *davening*. The rosh hayeshiva would not encroach upon the four *amos* that constituted his student's halachic "space."

   Later, the director, who all the time had been "sweating blood," asked whether, given the circumstances, the rosh hayeshiva could not have made an exception to the standards that he would normally demand of himself. The Rosh HaYeshiva explained that, for him, the *halachah* had erected an iron wall behind him. Short and frail as he was, he did not have the physical strength to breach such a barrier.

9. Since in the footnote on page 116 I allowed myself to take issue with an

ArtScroll rendition, I want to make up for it here. I suspect that many of you readers probably struggle every year, as I do, with *This year we are slaves; next year we will be free* in Ha Lachma Anya. We are not really "slaves," so why declare that we are?

I checked the ArtScroll Haggadah (transparency: the author is my brother-in-law, R. Yosef Elias) for its treatment of the issue. Here is a quote: *At present we might have civil rights, but spiritually we are slaves—in bondage to wrong ideas…*

Chapter 11

1. I would like to suggest that all of us might do well to train ourselves to be more concerned with the accuracy of the translations that we use and, in more general terms, that we devote some time to the study of how language behaves. I have found in my own learning that being awake to such issues can help. Please look at the last couple of pages in chapter 10, where I discuss the word *cheirus*. Please also see endnote 9 to that chapter.

    I checked (of course together with appropriate apologies), with a number of friends and colleagues, what they thought about during the *na'anu'im*. One hundred percent of my respondents admitted to chasing "evil spirits." Faced with such impressive unanimity, I began to wonder whether I am the one who is mistaken. However, on the basis of the Gemara that I am about to quote and the argument that I offer within, I am pretty sure that I got it right.

2. In the Greek and Roman periods it was customary to award the winner of chariot races with a palm frond as a mark of his supremacy. I imagine that cups or medals that are awarded today to the victors of various athletic events are direct descendants of those fronds.

    Here is some food for thought for those of you who are inclined to follow this up.

    R. Avin, (apparently an *amora* of the second or third generation—see Hyman's *Toldos Tana'im VeAmora'im*) seems to base his ideas concerning the *lulav's* symbolism upon his actual life experiences. In his time, if you were interested in finding out who had won a particular court case, all you had to do was to stand outside the courtroom and watch for the litigant who would come out carrying the palm frond.

    Is R. Avin implying that the palm frond was perceived as a sign of victory already when we stood at Sinai? Did Moshe Rabbeinu, when he shook his *arba minim*, make R. Avin's association? Was he celebrating the ascendancy of *klal Yisrael* over the *umos ha'olam* that had been attained on Rosh HaShanah?

    My admittedly cursory examination of the encyclopedias available to me (in which the "victory palm" is given due recognition) note that although it appears numberless times in illustrations that were made in Greek and Roman times, it does not appear even once until the late fifth century.

A number of possibilities occur to me. Here is one. R. Avin assumes that the usage that came into practice in the late fifth century would not have occurred in a vacuum. Somebody who was casting around for a suitable reward that could be used to recognize an athletic hero suddenly remembered that his Jewish neighbor was in the habit of waving around a decorated palm frond just after his New Year celebrations. Now why would he do that? It had never occurred to him to wonder about this before, but there is always a first time. He put two and two together and *presto!* the first Olympic "medal" was born. R. Avin decided that the enterprising and creative marketing genius who had thought this up had, in fact, hit upon the correct explanation.

I believe that there may also be a different way of understanding R. Avin, and for my purpose in writing this book it is of particular interest. I take it as a given that R. Avin would not have supposed that what was customary in his time would also have been the usage two thousand years earlier. This seems to me to be so obvious that it does not require any proof.

What then did he mean?

Perhaps it was a matter of taking the reality as it existed in his time and using it to imbue the actions that people were doing anyway, with a fresh meaning that would infuse their Yom Tov with new and wonderful reasons for being happy. The idea "Victory!" would be a natural for anybody who would see somebody carrying a *lulav*. It was an everyday phenomenon even when it was not Succos. R. Avin's *chidush* was to grab this ready-made symbol and to dress it up in a *Succos-dicke* garment. "We, too, have a legal victory to celebrate! It is not for nothing that Succos, the Time of Our Joy, comes right after Rosh Hashanah and Yom Kippur. It is true that the special joy of this *chag* is first and foremost stimulated by the end of the harvest cycle, the bringing home of last year's bounty, but it is up to us to translate that celebration of our physical blessings into an appreciation of the wonders that we have only recently experienced: the forgiving of our trespasses (Yom Kippur) and the cementing of our very special relationship with the Ribono shel Olam (our successful litigation on Rosh Hashanah). If in the past this latter aspect of Succos was less obvious to people because it lacked a tangible symbolism, now that we live in times in which the "victory palm" is a constant part of our lives, it has become an easily accessible thought!"

If there is some merit to this latter approach, it would be supportive of the approach that I am using throughout this book. As you all know very well by now, I have been trying to find ways in which things that we do all the time, more or less by rote, could be transformed into more meaningful exercises. For example, in chapter 3 I tried to find a message in *Elokai, Neshamah* to which I had not been awake before. Nowadays, when I remember to concentrate, it helps me a lot. Now I am fully aware that I cannot possibly claim that what I suggested is *the* meaning. At best it is *a* meaning. If my second suggestion in this note is correct, that would give my efforts a stronger legitimization than it had had till now.

1. I am aware of the fact that there are also laws in the Torah that we do not understand. They do not disturb me at all. These are *mitzvos* that the Ribono shel Olam handed down to us without explanation. He has the authority to command us at will and it is not our place to question Him. The beating of the *aravos* is different. It is a *minhag nevi'im* (Succah 41a). That means that the prophets who functioned in the early years of the second Beis HaMikdash sat down around a table and, for reasons unknown to us, decided to create a new custom with which everybody would be expected to comply. It would take the form of banging an *aravah* on the floor.

    I cannot imagine that such an edict would have been issued without a discussion. What possible religious value would be furthered by such a strange act? I am quite sure that whoever had made that suggestion would have had to argue his case and to demonstrate to his peers the sheer rightness of the mooted ceremony.

    I have not been able to find any record of what he said. I looked around carefully on my search program, but with the exception of short references in the *sifrei kabbalah* of which, unsurprisingly, I understood nothing at all, I drew a blank.

    Subsequently in *Machzor HaMikdash* by Yisrael Ariel I came across a reference to R. Tzemach Gaon who is said to have claimed that since the lip-shaped *aravah* stands for speech, it can be said that the practice was instituted to bring atonement for sins that we may have committed when indulging in forbidden speech. This idea might be hinted at in Eichah 3:29: *And he will place his mouth in the dust, perhaps there will be hope*, in which *his mouth* would be the *aravah* and *the dust* would be the ground upon which the *aravah* is banged.

    R. Ariel notes that this approach would not explain why this practice should belong specifically to Succos. That, I believe, can be answered. As we shall presently learn from the *Sefas Emes*, Hoshana Rabba (Dovid HaMelech's special day, see within) is specifically, and more than any other day, devoted to *tefillah*. It would stand to reason that, on such an auspicious occasion, we would want to cleanse our mouths from the filth of our transgressions, in order that our entreaties might find more ready acceptance.

2. The following needs to be stressed.

    In the previous note we learned of R. Tzemach Gaon's ideas. As we go along in our explorations we will be spending time with the Sefas Emes's explanations concerning the nature of Hoshana Rabba. Both offer their thoughts based on the assumption that it is the *aravah* that is banged. That is, of course, our practice. The thoughts that I will offer are also based upon that assumption.

    However, there is another opinion in the Mishnah (Succah 45a). R. Yochanan ben Berokah does not agree with our practice. He opines that not *aravos* but *palm-branches* (according to Rashi) were beaten. He goes so far as to record that Hoshana Rabba used to be called *Yom Chibut Charayos* (*the day when palm branches are beaten*). Now there is nothing problematic about such a difference of opinion. It is not different from any other of the disagreements that fill the entire Talmud. However, it *does* require that we realize that any explanation for the practice of the beating based upon the nature of the *aravah* as hinting at speech will not hold well for R. Yochanan's practice.

We must remember then that all that is being said in this chapter may hold well for our banging the *aravos*. They cannot be used to explain the concept of the beating in an abstract sense that would be applicable to, let us say, *lulavim*.

3. Having worked so hard on trying to understand something of the awesome *avodah* of the beating of the *aravos*, I find it difficult to simply let it go. It goes against nature to permit something so beautiful and holy to end up as a discard. I go through the same pangs of parting on every Hoshana Rabba. There has got to be a better way.

Well, there is. We don't simply throw out the *aravah* after we have *geklapped* it. Reverently, we lay it aside so that, in half a year's time, we will be able to use it as fuel for next year's matzah baking (see *Rama* 665:9).

Is there any logic to this custom that seems to have developed on its own?

If the suggestions that I have made in this chapter have merit, then the answer is a mighty "Yes!" What, after all, is matzah if not the *lechem oni*, the bread associated with much speech (see Pesachim 115b). Do you get it!? If, in preparation for Shemini Atzeres and Simchas Torah, we have been able to move ourselves (at least in theory) into the speechless world, that is not in a spirit of permanently degrading speech. Come Pesach, the *aravah* will have received its consolation prize. It can't wait for the matzah baking to begin! If Hoshana Rabba is the day of ultimate speechlessness, Pesach is the Yom Tov of speech!

The following should be noted. We have recorded Rama's opinion that the *aravos* are to be stored till the next *erev* Pesach so that they can be used in the matzah-baking process. I have no explanation for the fact that in Orech Chaim 445:7 the *Mishnah Berurah* recommends that if *hoshanos* are available, these should be used for BURNING THE *chametz* and makes no mention of the fact that Rama suggests that they should be used for BAKING THE *matzos*.

Subsequently I saw that the Gaon, R. Chaim Kanievsky in his *Shone Halachos* asks this question in both places, but offers no answer.

There is another point that ought to be raised. We have just learned that the *hoshanos* need to be treated with respect even after they have served their purpose. Directions concerning what to do with them (have the coming Pesach in mind!) are provided. The minor problem (R. Kanievsky uses the term *A little further investigation is required*) of the apparent contradiction that we have just discussed is unfortunate, but it does not in any way touch upon the principle that is involved. Everybody agrees that the *hoshana* ought to be preserved for the coming *erev* Pesach.

What about the *arba minim*? Why is there no mention about what is to be done with them once they are no longer required for the *na'anu'im*? As far as I could discover, there is not even a whisper that it were well to preserve at least the *aravos* for next Pesach? Why treat the *hoshanos* differently than the *aravos* that served for the *na'anu'im*?

It seems clear to me that nothing needed to be said concerning the fate of the *arba minim* because they fall naturally into the same category as the worn-out tzitzis, to the disposal of which an entire *chapter* (21) is devoted. They have the same characteristics (they were used for a mitzvah but carried no *kedushah*). As a result, *Some authorities maintain that once they are no longer being used [for the* mitzvah*], one should not treat them disrespectfully and simply throw them out. However, it is not required that they be formally stored (as, for example torn siddurim). However, if someone is moved to store them formally, he will surely be blessed* (Rama, there).

So why is the *hoshana* special?

I think that all this seems to confirm the validity of what I have suggested in this chapter. With the *"geklappte hoshana"* it is not simply a matter of having reached a point at which it is no longer required. The *hoshana* was beaten to the ground; it was actively rejected. Its self-respect must be restored. *Klal Yisrael*, in its acute sensitivity for what might be pleasing in the eyes of the Ribono shel Olam, thought up the precisely appropriate prophylactic. Already on Hoshana Rabba we can look forward to Pesach when speech, by way of the *matzos*, will once more come into its own.

Chapter 13

1. Try to imagine the following story.

Let us assume that our friend Reuven, whom, together with his occasional adversary, Shimon, we know so well from countless *sugios* in the Gemara, lives in New York. He has a store, makes a reasonable living, and is blessed with a large and beautiful family ranging from kindergartners through the outer reaches of high school and beyond. One day his wife comes home from a *shiur* and suggests that it seems ridiculous to live in *galus* by choice. "Let us pull up our roots and move to Eretz Yisrael!"

Reuven is not only a responsible wage-earner, but he is also the perfect husband. He takes his wife's idea seriously and they start thinking. All you readers will have no difficulty in filling in the blanks. It is a decision that should not be, indeed cannot be, taken lightly.

Can we imagine the following dénouement?

One evening Reuven rushes in, all excited. He calls out to his wife, "You know what?! The decision is made. As I came in I kissed the mezuzah and it suddenly struck me. If the Ribono shel Olam, Who is so great, can stand guard over us who are so very much less than that, for sure we ought to move."

They packed. They left and lived happily ever after.

You get the point. The Onkelos story can use some deeper analysis.

2. Maharal asserts that a king protects his people. *For it is for this he is king— that he guards his nation.* I am not sure how to understand *For it is for this.* It could be a matter of definition: it lies in the nature of a king to protect his people, or it might be a matter of duty: it is incumbent upon a king to protect his people. Either way, at the time of this writing I have not been able to find a source for this assertion.

Within the context of our discussion in this chapter, it occurred to me that the king looks after his people because he needs them: *There is no king without a nation.* However, I have not been able to find a direct source for this statement in Chazal. The references available to me identify various *sefarim* in which it is quoted, but, again, no open Chazal.

The closest I got was a quote from R. Elchanan Wasserman in *Kovetz Shiurim*:

R. Elchanan is uncertain about the status of a king who had been forcefully and illegally deposed from his throne. Does the illegality of the deposal leave him with his status as king untouched, or does the principle that there is no king without a nation make it impossible for him to retain his status?

He cites a Yerushalmi at Horios 3:2 that appears to come down on the side of the second of the two options. Here is the background. If someone inadvertently transgresses a prohibition that would carry the *kares* punishment had the transgression been intentional, he is obliged to bring a *chat'os* sacrifice. That obligation is universal, but there are gradations concerning what animal is to be brought. A king brings a male goat while the commoner brings a female. The Yerushalmi discusses the issue of what animal King David would have had to bring had he sinned during the six months of civil war when he was fleeing from his rebellious son, Avshalom. The Yerushalmi records that he would have been treated as a commoner and therefore brought a female goat.

The Yerushalmi is clearly a legitimate source for the second option. There is no king without a nation.

Chapter 14

1. I imagine that the active form *And you shall tie (U'keshartam)* used for the tefillin *shel yad,* in contrast to the passive *And it shall be (Vehayu)* used for the tefillin *shel rosh,* derives from the fact that the tefillin of the hand is covered and cannot be seen (*It is a sign for you, not a sign for others*) while the tefillin of the head is out in the open (*And all of the nations shall see...*). Once

covered, our relationship to the *shel yad* derives only from the fact that we remember tying it on. The *shel rosh* fulfills its purpose by simply "being" where it is supposed to be.

2. Herewith I offer some general thoughts about the mezuzah. Much of what I am writing in this and the other chapters that deal with this topic take the information in this note for granted.

   In the course of the current and the following chapter we will discover that, in spite of certain similarities between tefillin and the mezuzah, at essence they fill very different functions. The tefillin are transformative. Ideally the *Shechinah* rests upon the person who wears them and, apparently, for as long as they are upon him, his very personality is meant to undergo an infusion of the sacred. (See Berachos 6a: *And all of the nations of the land shall see that the Name of HaShem is upon you, and they will fear you...these are the tefillin that are worn on the head.*) Accordingly, the tefillin deal with "being." The mezuzah does not aspire, in and of itself, to create a new person. It, so to speak, fuses into the very structure of the house. It becomes a part of, really an extension of, the doorpost. It is educational rather than creative.

Chapter 15

1. The story is told that the authorities once decided to arrest the Vilna Gaon. They brought him to the police station where he found out that they were about to parade him through the town, so that the Vilna lowlifes could have some fun with him. The Gaon decided that he was not obliged by the Torah to allow himself to be so degraded. Accordingly he took his tallis off his head, thereby uncovering his *tefillin shel rosh*. His captors became terrified and fell over each other in their determination to escape.

2. Somehow, I am scared to write the following in the body of this chapter. Back here, where anyway a lot of readers do not venture, things are a little more private and it is easier to make the following suggestion—just between ourselves.

   Yesterday I attended the bar mitzvah of a particularly bright and promising young man and it was a sheer delight to listen to his *p'shetel* and then to the many speeches describing the stellar future that awaited him and exhorting him to take seriously his new status as one fully obligated to obey all the *mitzvos*. With tefillin weighing heavily on my mind because I was in the middle of this chapter, I allowed my mind to wonder (and wander) what might be a useful message to offer this gifted young man. I looked around the room that was packed with truly wonderful people and I found myself questioning how many times in their entire lives, given the Rambam's standards, any of these people had worn his tefillin as they apparently demand to be worn.

   What future, at least in the world of tefillin that was so central to our bar mitzvah boy's thinking during that really uplifting Shabbos, awaited him?

Would he twenty or thirty years down the road look back, bemused and horrified, and ask himself whether he had ever *really* worn his tefillin in the way that the Ribono shel Olam had in mind?

I decided, in a purely theoretical way, that, given the opportunity, I would speak to him as follows.

My Dear bar mitzvah:

Try to imagine that, instead of celebrating your bar mitzvah on Yeshiva Lane in twenty-first-century America, you would have lived two hundred years ago in the Polish village from which your family stems. You can figure out that things would have been very, very different. Among other things, you would certainly not have been wearing that beautiful new black hat of which you are so rightfully proud. But seriously, think of all the advantages you have by living here and now. Limitless choices of the yeshivos you might attend, and planes to take you there, every sefer that you might possibly need available to you, and so on and on and on. Lucky you!

There is, however, one thing that back then you would have had, and which, sadly, you are missing now.

Let me explain.

Let us imagine that President Obama would wake up one morning and decide that he is not getting enough respect from people. He has a great idea. He invites a famous jeweler to the White House and orders himself a crown. It is going to be the fanciest crown, that anybody ever wore. He just knows in his bones that once he wears that crown all his problems will be solved. Everybody will render him the respect that is his due.

You can imagine what would happen. The cartoonists would have enough material to keep them busy for a year and the GNP would drop because nobody would be working since everybody would be rolling on the floor laughing their heads off.

It ain't gonna work!

Why not?

Because we live in a culture in which crowns can't cut the ice. They did very well in a culture in which there was a concept of *nobility*. There was a time when not all people were born equal. There were certain families that were thought of as being special. They were somehow better, somehow more deserving of honor than were other people. Never mind trying to understand the theories upon which such a system was based. It doesn't matter because the whole concept has long since disappeared. As long as it lasted, crowns did a good job. They worked as a symbol. They identified the person who was entitled to wear one as a member of the nobility. But, no nobility, no crowns. Today they just look ridiculous. Poor Mr. Obama!

However, at least as far as the members of the nobility were concerned, there was one advantage that really mattered. People used a French expression to describe it. Here is the expression: noblesse oblige. It means that nobility carries responsibility with it. If, indeed, you are to be deserving of the honor that you demand from others, you have to be an honorable person, one who deserves, or better, has earned, the right to be honored. Standards of behavior will be expected of you that would not be asked of others. Nobility comes wrapped in very real obligations.

What does all this have to do with you and your bar mitzvah?

I'll tell you. One of the most exciting things about becoming bar mitzvah is that you get to put on tefillin every day. The Tur tells us that, up to the *berachah*, "*oter Yisrael b'sif'arah*," his father, the Rosh, used to say *Birkas HaShachar* without wearing tefillin. At that point he stopped, put on his tefillin, and then said the *berachah*. Here is why. Berachos 60b teaches us that this *berachah* is to be said every morning when we put on our hats. See, we are back at your nice black hat once more. But there is also an inner meaning. Look at the word, *tif'arah*. You see that the root word is *pe'er*, which means *a crown*. Now there is a *pasuk* in Yechezkel (20:17) where the Ribono shel Olam refers to tefillin as *pe'er*. Apparently tefillin can be looked upon as though they were a crown. So the *berachah* can be understood as meaning, Blessed is the Ribono shel Olam Who *crowns Yisrael with* tefillin. That is why the Rosh chose to organize his *Birkas HaShachar* as he did. It turns out that tefillin are a "crown" and when we wear them, we are "kings."

If we are kings, then we are nobles. If we are nobles, we are bound by the rule that noblesse oblige. If that is so then we can understand all the demands that the Rambam (*Tefillin* 4:25) makes on us. He is very strict about the kind of person we ought to be while we are wearing tefillin. And that being so you can now understand why I said earlier that there is one advantage that you would have had if you would have had your bar mitzvah back in Poland two hundred years ago. You would have been living in a society in which ideas like "kingship," "nobility," "the responsibilities that nobility imposes upon people who claim to be nobles" would have been part of everyday life and would therefore have been very clear to you. Above all, you would have had a great deal of respect for a person who is wearing a crown—which from today onwards is going to be *you* every morning when you put on tefillin—and you would have felt yourself governed by noblesse oblige. In practical terms, that means that you would have taken Rambam's exhortation seriously. You would *takke* have made sure to be precisely the kind of person whom the Rambam defines.

But you are not in Poland; you are here. It is not two hundred years ago; it is now. So it has become very difficult to understand the responsibility that wearing tefillin puts on us.

So I want to give you a bar mitzvah present—not a *sefer* and most certainly not an iPod, but a bit of advice. Try to get into the habit that when you take your tefillin out of their bag in the morning, you don't put them on right away. Give yourself a little while—say about a minute—to think about the following. "I am about to put on a crown. That means I am about to become a temporary king. That is a very big responsibility. A king who does not act like a king is a great big failure. Now I don't exactly know how kings feel or act. Still I know enough to know that I cannot be the way I usually am; I have got to be a whole lot better. I will try. I will try very, very hard!"

I suspect that if you really try seriously to get into this habit, then, twenty-five years from now, if you look back on your life, you will have more satisfaction than many other people who never educated themselves into that sense of responsibility.

Chapter 16

1. If you believe that another metaphor might help, you can think of a de-flated balloon. You can blow it up and its potential will be fully realized. Left limp, it is still a total balloon full of promise if not of air.

2. I cannot resist the temptation of sharing the following true anecdote with you. A highly regarded and highly successful professional in a certain community surprised all his friends and neighbors by deciding to spend his entire morning in Torah study, pursuing his other commitments only after lunch.

   There was a story behind that decision. The man had a son who was not particularly motivated in his learning. He was a slacker. After a revolving-door sequence of top-notch *rebbeim* had been hired without success to help the youngster, the father decided to have a serious talk with the boy about his attitude. Why, he wanted to know, was he so little motivated?

   In the uncomplicated teenage wisdom of our children, the answer came fast and furious: "If Torah learning is so important, how come I hardly ever see you cracking a Gemara?"

   The father was sufficiently wise to draw the required conclusion.

   The "cliché" ending of this story would be that today the young man has become one of the top *roshei yeshiva* in Bnei Brak. I cannot either confirm or deny this conclusion. I simply do not know. But the story stands on its own. It does not need any ending, cliché or otherwise. I feel pretty good about my suggestion for the *peshat* in our *pasuk*. What do you think?

3. I have been careful to limit what I have written here to the tefillin *shel rosh* that is meant to be clearly visible to everybody. The tefillin *shel yad*, to the contrary, is meant to be covered. See Menachos 37b: *It is a sign for* YOU, *and not a sign for others*. If we combine this *halachah* with the one that the Gemara works out at Menachos 36a, *At all times that [the* tefillin *is worn] between your eyes, there should be two [objects worn]*, the *shel rosh* is to be donned only *after* the *shel yad* is already in place, everything fits in nicely with the theory that we are propounding here.

   This as follows: It is precisely as we have said. Tefilin have the function of permitting us to make our love of the Ribono shel Olam known even beyond our family circle, within the public arena. That is to be accomplished by the "crown" character of the tefillin *shel rosh* (see next note). However, there is a problem. Anybody can put on a tefillin *shel rosh* and parade around in public, but not everybody is worthy to function as ambassador for the Ribono shel Olam. Before he assumes that function, he has to internalize the lessons that he is about to teach. This is the function of the tefillin *shel yad* that must therefore precede the *shel rosh*. Modestly covered, invisible to all but to our own hearts, it whispers its private messages to us. Only after that are we ready to go public.

The two tefillin function in tandem, the first preparing us for the second. If only we thought all these ideas through as we put on our tefillin every morning! Perhaps you would like to reread the bar mitzvah speech that I offered in endnote 3 of the last chapter. *Oy!* We can all use a little *mussar!*

If you have access to the Hirsch Chumash, you might want to read his commentary to the tefillin in *VaEschanan*. It can make the entire experience of putting on the tefillin more meaningful to you.

4. How do the tefillin work their magic?

Easy! They turn us into kings and, as we learned in endnote 3 of the previous chapter, *create in us noblesse oblige*.

And how do they turn us into kings?

Easy! Yechezkel 24:7 uses *pe'er* to describe tefillin and *pe'er* is a crown. Kings wear crowns, right? It follows; you wear a crown, you are a king! Once more: Easy!

True! But things are not quite so simple. Isn't it a truism that if everybody is a king, nobody is a king?

That is a reasonable question. However, you notice that I used "reasonable," not "good." Your question grows from insufficient linguistic intuition. Before you wondered who the subjects might be, you should have questioned the original premise. Things do not become "crowns" simply by calling them crowns. *Tefillin* are clearly objects of religious significance; real crowns speak of the power of a ruler. Where is the connection?

Right you are! So where is the connection?

At this point we are going to have to learn a little *Kuzari*. I will make this digression as short as possible and get back to the tefillin as fast as possible. But, given our subject, digress we must. You will find that it was all worthwhile. The following is a paraphrase of the Third Essay in the *Kuzari* 2–5.

2. The Kuzari said: "Please tell me what behavior would be expected from someone who aspires to achieve the state of Chasidus, *saintliness*."
3. The Rabbi said: "He would have to be concerned for the welfare of his country. He would want to be sure to provide all the citizens with their needs. His governance would be based upon justice, he would eschew oppression and control the provisions that are available to him such that nobody would get more than he deserves. By ruling thus, he would win the loyalty of his subjects, all of whom will gladly fulfill his requests and obey his orders. Moreover he will be able to freely criticize them. They will take his admonishments seriously."

4. The Kuzari said: "You got me all wrong! I was interested in how a Chasid might act; you, however, have defined a successful ruler."

5. The Rabbi said: "You do not understand. To be a Chasid one must be a ruler. He must be able to exact finely honed discipline from all his senses. His faculties must subordinate themselves to his wishes in precisely the way that the king's servants stand ready to do his bidding in all matters. For practical purposes he is their king.

In number 6 the Kuzari goes on to explain the *nimshal* to his *mashal* in great detail. The upshot of his presentation is to demonstrate that saintliness = control. It can be defined as being a ruler over his physical needs and drives.

And that is the "crown power" of the *tefillin shel rosh*. By now we are all familiar with the fact that this tefillin is the reminder that *the name of HaShem is called upon you*, that the Ribono shel Olam marks us as His own.

IN RECOGNITION OF A

GENEROUS CONTRIBUTION

IN MEMORY

OF

Dr. Richard

&

Regina Weinberger

OF

VIENNA, AUSTRIA

AND

BALTIMORE, MARYLAND

IN MEMORY

OF

OUR BELOVED

HUSBAND, FATHER,

AND

TEACHER

Solomon Ralph Bijou

HE LIT A LIGHT IN OUR HEARTS

THAT

WILL GUIDE US AND OUR CHILDREN

THROUGHOUT OUR LIVES.

—FROM HIS WIFE,

CHILDREN, GRANDCHILDREN,

AND

GREAT-GRANDCHILDREN

IN LOVING MEMORY

OF

Esther & Isaac Mezrahi

PILLARS OF OUR COMMUNITY,

THEY ALWAYS KNEW WHAT HAD TO BE DONE

AND, PROFOUNDLY CREATIVE,

FOUND WAYS TO DO IT.

ABOVE ALL THEY WERE A TEAM.

ONE HEART

ANIMATED THEM BOTH,

ONE SOUL

BREATHED LIFE INTO THEIR DREAMS.

AFTER FATHER PASSED ON,

MOTHER KEPT THE FLAME BURNING

FOR EIGHTEEN MORE YEARS.

MAY THEIR MEMORY BE A BLESSING

FOR US, OUR CHILDREN, AND GRANDCHILDREN.

THERE ARE MANY PEOPLE WHO OWE

THEIR LIVES TO

THE LOVING CONCERN OF

Ezra & Zekia Shasho

OF BLESSED MEMORY.

WE GRATEFULLY RECALL THEIR GOODNESS

AND

THE WONDERFUL EXAMPLE THAT THEY SET.

THEY, AS ALSO

THEIR BELOVED DAUGHTER

Frieda Kredy

AND THEIR BELOVED SON

Egal Shasho

OF BLESSED MEMORY,

WILL FOREVER LIVE ON IN OUR HEARTS.

—BY THEIR CHILDREN,

GRANDCHILDREN, AND FAMILY

Albert Hamway זצ"ל

UNDERSTOOD WHAT JEWISH LIVING

WAS ALL ABOUT.

IN FARAWAY JAPAN HE RAISED HIS CHILDREN

WITH A LOVE FOR THEIR TRADITION.

THEY EACH BUILT

WARM AND LOVING JEWISH HOMES,

PASSING ON TO THEIR CHILDREN AND

THEY TO THEIRS THE FLAME

WHICH THEIR FATHER HAD PASSED TO THEM.

HE IS REMEMBERED WITH LOVE BY

HIS WIFE, HIS CHILDREN,

GRANDCHILDREN,

AND GREAT-GRANDCHILDREN.

מציבים אנו בזה

מזכרת נצח

לאבינו מורנו היקר

ר' לטמן

בן ר' חיים דוב בער ז"ל

איש צנוע

שכל חייו רץ כצבי

לעשות רצון אבינו שבשמים

ולאמנו מורתנו היקרה

רות רבקה לאה

בת ר' אברהם ע"ה

יהא זכרם ברוך

IN LOVING MEMORY

OF

OUR PARENTS

Mollie

AND

Sam E. Levy

IN LOVING MEMORY

OF MY BELOVED PARENTS,

AND

MORE, MY GOOD AND PRECIOUS

FRIENDS

Jack & Jeanette Feldman

THEY WERE GENEROUS, WARMHEARTED,

AND GENTLE.

YOU COULD NOT MEET THEM

WITHOUT BEING TOUCHED BY THEIR

GOODNESS.

WITH A SMILE ON HIS WISE FACE

AND NOVHARDOK MUSSAR IN HIS HEART

HaRav Chaim Mordechai Weinkrantz זצ"ל

UNDERSTOOD US ALL SO WELL, SO VERY WELL.

NO PROBLEM,

BUT HIS WISDOM FOUND A SOLUTION.

NO PAIN, BUT HIS EMPATHY

WAS A HEALING BALM.

CHILD OF A CULTURE VERY DIFFERENT

FROM OUR OWN, HE NEVERTHELESS FOUND

COMMONALITY IN HIS AND OUR

JEWISH HEARTS.

WE WILL NEVER FORGET THE BOOKS

WHICH HE SO DILIGENTLY TAUGHT US,

NOR THE LIFE LESSONS

FOR WHICH HE WAS A LIVING TEXT.

—THE MONDAY SHIUR

TWO WONDERFUL PEOPLE

ONE LOVING HEART

Ally & Marlow Dayon

KNEW HOW LIFE WAS SUPPOSED TO BE LIVED

QUIETLY AND MODESTLY

THEY WENT ABOUT THEIR ACTS OF CARING

HELPING WHERE HELP WAS NEEDED

COAXING SMILES FROM BROKEN HEARTS

WITH THEIR COLORFUL AND BUBBLY NATURES

THEIR DOOR WAS ALWAYS OPEN

AS WERE ALSO THEIR MINDS

THEIRS WAS THE WISDOM OF THE HEART

THEY ENJOYED LIFE AND ENJOYED EACH OTHER

WE MISS THEM SADLY BUT OUR PRIDE IN WHO

OUR PARENTS WERE SOFTENS OUR PAIN

BY THEIR DAUGHTER SHARON GROSSBERG

AND THEIR SONS

IRWIN, RICHARD AND JEFFERY

DAYON

לזכות רפואה שלמה

צופיה בת רות

ותזכה

לחיים ארוכים חיים של שלום חיים של טובה

חיים של ברכה

וחיים של חלוץ עצמות

יהי רצון שתזכה לברכה והצלחה בכל אשר תפנה

ותהיה לרוב נחת

לכל אוהביה